P9-BUG-680

Battered by high seas and a northwesterly gale, two German U-boats on patrol in mid-Atlantic meet unexpectedly in the winter of 1941. The chance encounter surprised both boats, which had been fighting the storm for over a week. Journalist Lothar-Günther Buchheim, sent on patrol with the U-96 (in foreground), took this picture evoking the perilous life of Germany's sea wolves.

THE BATTLE OF THE ATLANTIC

Other Publications:

THE SEAFARERS
THE ENCYCLOPEDIA OF COLLECTIBLES
THE GREAT CITIES
HOME REPAIR AND IMPROVEMENT
THE WORLD'S WILD PLACES
THE TIME-LIFE LIBRARY OF BOATING
HUMAN BEHAVIOR
THE ART OF SEWING
THE OLD WEST
THE EMERGENCE OF MAN
THE AMERICAN WILDERNESS
THE TIME-LIFE ENCYCLOPEDIA OF GARDENING
LIFE LIBRARY OF PHOTOGRAPHY
THIS FABULOUS CENTURY
FOODS OF THE WORLD
TIME-LIFE LIBRARY OF AMERICA
TIME-LIFE LIBRARY OF ART
GREAT AGES OF MAN
LIFE SCIENCE LIBRARY
THE LIFE HISTORY OF THE UNITED STATES
TIME READING PROGRAM
LIFE NATURE LIBRARY
LIFE WORLD LIBRARY
FAMILY LIBRARY
- HOW THINGS WORK IN YOUR HOME
- THE TIME-LIFE BOOK OF THE FAMILY CAR
- THE TIME-LIFE FAMILY LEGAL GUIDE
- THE TIME-LIFE BOOK OF FAMILY FINANCE

Previous World War II Volumes:

Prelude to War
Blitzkrieg
The Battle of Britain
The Rising Sun

WORLD WAR II · TIME-LIFE BOOKS · ALEXANDRIA, VIRGINIA

BY BARRIE PITT
AND THE EDITORS OF TIME-LIFE BOOKS

THE BATTLE OF THE ATLANTIC

WORLD WAR II

Editorial Staff for *The Battle of the Atlantic*
Editor: William K. Goolrick
Picture Editor/Designer: Thomas S. Huestis
Text Editors: Thomas H. Flaherty Jr., Anne Horan
Staff Writers: Richard W. Flanagan, Henry P. Leifermann, Sterling Seagrave
Researchers: Jane Edwin, Barbara Fleming, Clara Nicolai, Robin Richman
Editorial Assistant: Dolores Morrissy

Editorial Production
Production Editor: Douglas B. Graham
Operations Manager: Gennaro C. Esposito
Assistant Production Editor: Feliciano Madrid
Quality Control: Robert L. Young (director), James J. Cox (assistant), Michael G. Wight (associate)
Art Coordinator: Anne B. Landry
Copy Staff: Susan B. Galloway (chief), Margery duMond, Victoria Lee, Florence Keith, Celia Beattie
Picture Department: Dolores A. Littles, Barbara S. Simon

Correspondents: Elisabeth Kraemer (Bonn); Margot Hapgood, Dorothy Bacon (London); Susan Jonas, Lucy T. Voulgaris (New York); Maria Vincenza Aloisi (Paris); Ann Natanson (Rome). Valuable assistance was also provided by Carolyn T. Chubet, Miriam Hsia (New York).

The Author: BARRIE PITT is the author of two books on naval history, and also wrote *1918—The Last Act,* an account of the final year of World War I. He was the editor of the eight-volume *Histories of the First and Second World Wars* published in Great Britain, and the editor-in-chief of a paperback series, *Ballantine's Illustrated History of World War II.*

The Consultants: COL. JOHN R. ELTING, USA (Ret.), is a military historian, author of *The Battle of Bunker's Hill, A Military History* and *Atlas of the Napoleonic Wars.* He edited *Military Uniforms in North America: The Revolutionary Era* and was associate editor of *The West Point Atlas of American Wars.*

HENRY H. ADAMS is a retired Navy captain who served aboard the destroyer U.S.S. *Owen* in the major campaigns of the Central Pacific during World War II. A native of Ann Arbor, Michigan, he was graduated from the University of Michigan, and received his M.A. and Ph.D. degrees from Columbia University. After his service in World War II he was a professor at the U.S. Naval Academy in Annapolis, Maryland, and was later head of the English Department at Illinois State University. His books include *1942: The Year That Doomed the Axis, Years of Deadly Peril, Years of Expectation, Years to Victory* and *Harry Hopkins: A Biography.*

HANS-ADOLF JACOBSEN, Director of the Seminar for Political Science at the University of Bonn, is the co-author of *Anatomy of the S.S.,* and editor of *Decisive Battles of World War II: The German View.*

DONALD MACINTYRE served with the Royal Navy during World War II as a commander of destroyers and convoy escort groups in the North Atlantic. He was awarded the Distinguished Service Order three times, the Distinguished Service Cross and the American Legion of Merit. Since his retirement in 1954 he has written more than a score of books on naval historical subjects, including *U-Boat Killer* and *Narvik.*

Second printing. Revised 1978.
Published simultaneously in Canada.
Library of Congress catalogue card number 77-74822.
School and library distribution by Silver Burdett Company, Morristown, New Jersey.

CHAPTERS

PICTURE ESSAYS

CONTENTS

THE BATTLE'S FIRST VICTIMS

The British aircraft carrier Courageous, torpedoed off Ireland by a German U-boat, heels over before sinking on September 17, 1939, with a loss of 518 lives.

THE TORPEDOES TAKE THEIR TOLL

Regent Tiger: *November 21, 1939. Black smoke billows up from the burning British tanker as she starts to sink just after being torpedoed.*

The last months of 1939 were widely described as the time of the "phony war"; after Poland fell, there was little land fighting anywhere. But it was different at sea. There, the war raged with a fury that presaged a long, bloody conflict.

Not 10 hours after Prime Minister Neville Chamberlain's announcement that war had begun, a U-boat torpedoed the British liner *Athenia*. Of the 1,400 passengers aboard (many of whom were fleeing the war in Europe), 112 lost their lives, including 28 Americans.

In the weeks that followed, Hitler's sea wolves—as his submarine force was called—struck time and again at the merchant shipping so vital to Britain's economic survival. Even British warships fell prey to submarine sorties. The first big casualty was the aircraft carrier *Courageous* in September, followed within a month by the battleship *Royal Oak*.

The losses of matériel were appalling, but what happened to the crews and passengers stunned all who heard of their fate. In the frightful minutes between a torpedo's hull-rending crash and the stricken vessel's death plunge, those who were not killed outright by the explosion often were crushed by collapsing steel, scalded to death by steam from ruptured boilers, or drowned by the inrushing sea. When there was fire, survivors often faced another kind of torture, struggling in water whose surface was aflame with oil.

While the torpedoes wreaked massive destruction, magnetic mines—laid in large numbers along coastal waterways by submarines, surface ships and the Luftwaffe—took a terrible toll of their own. At the same time, in more distant waters, powerful raiders like the pocket battleship *Graf Spee* were blasting victims out of the sea.

By the end of 1939, the box score on the Battle of the Atlantic had mounted frighteningly. Within the short space of four months, U-boats, mines, airplanes and surface raiders had sent more than 215 merchant ships—a staggering 748,000 tons of shipping—to the bottom, along with two of Britain's largest warships. More than 1,500 lives had been lost—and it was clear that despite the lull on land, a long war lay ahead on the world's waters.

Athenia: *September 3, 1939. A U-boat casualty off Scotland on the first day of the War, the doomed British liner begins to settle by the stern.*

Gipsy: November 22, 1939. *The British destroyer sinks off the English coast after hitting a mine while going to the rescue of three downed Nazi airmen.*

Doric Star: December 2, 1939. *The 10,086-ton British freighter explodes amidships after being fired upon by the German raider Graf Spee.*

San Galisto: December 2, 1939. *Escape ladders dangle from the deck of the British tanker as she sinks off the English coast, the victim of two mines.*

Aragonite: November 22, 1939. *With only her funnel and masts above water, the British minesweeper becomes another mine fatality off England.*

Royal Oak: October 14, 1939. *The World War I battleship, seen in a prouder moment, became a U-boat victim at Scapa Flow with the loss of 833 aboard.*

1

The brilliant exploit of the U-47
Unrestricted sub warfare begins
The threat to Britain's lifeline
Britain's careful preparations for the wrong war
A machine that listened underwater
The great U-boat shortage
A master submariner's plan
Hitler vs. the German Navy
Helpful clues from a mislaid mine
French nests for German subs

UNLEASHING THE SEA WOLVES

Shortly after 7 o'clock on the evening of October 13, 1939, off the Orkney Islands, the waters of the North Sea parted above the rising conning tower of the German submarine *U-47*, and a few seconds later the hatch was thrown back. Lieut. Commander Günther Prien, one of the most promising of Hitler's U-boat commanders, tense after a day spent on the bottom, pulled himself up onto the bridge. As he did so, he suppressed an oath.

Nature had played an infuriating trick. Although weather conditions were perfect, as had been predicted—a moonless night, choppy but not boisterous seas and a fresh breeze—all was apparently ruined by that spectacular freak of arctic lighting, the aurora borealis. Billows of colorful light streamed across the northern skies, illuminating one half of the horizon and threatening to betray the presence of the submarine.

Briefly, Prien considered abandoning his mission. But weeks would pass before ideal conditions of tide and moon would prevail again. Moreover, the high morale that had crackled through the *U-47* since he had briefed his men on their mission might be impossible to recapture.

For the 31-year-old Prien, the *U-47* was his first command and this was his first big assignment. He had been chosen by Commodore Karl Dönitz, head of the German submarine arm, to carry out the first special U-boat operation of the War: an audacious attack on the British fleet right in the middle of its home base at Scapa Flow.

In all of World War II, no U-boat commander would be asked to perform a more daring or difficult mission. Scapa Flow, a deepwater, almost landlocked basin in the Orkney Islands, was one of the most heavily guarded anchorages in the world. Its entrances were blocked by sunken ships, mines and nets, and patrolled by the Royal Navy. Moreover, a submarine attempting to sneak in was likely to encounter exceptionally heavy currents.

Scapa Flow held a special, bitter significance for the Germans. The main units of the German fleet had been interned there after World War I. In 1919, while the Allies were arguing over the final disposition of the fleet, the skeleton German crews that were manning the ships scuttled and sank most of them.

Now the Germans were returning to Scapa Flow. Dönitz himself had planned the operation, studying aerial photographs to find the best route into the anchorage, and personally picking Prien to lead the attack (he reminded Prien, as he did so, that in World War I, two German submarines had attempted a similar attack on the British fleet in Scapa Flow, and had not returned).

On the morning of October 8, the *U-47* slipped from her mooring at Kiel in northern Germany and passed through the Kiel Canal into the North Sea. The crew members were still in the dark as to the nature of their mission, but suspicions that it was something special were aroused when the U-boat spotted a pall of smoke on the horizon and Prien ordered a dive without even investigating. Only when the submarine was lying on the surface not far from the Orkneys, recharging her batteries and renewing her supply of compressed air, did Prien break the news to his first watch officer, Engelbert Endrass. "Hold onto something, Endrass," he said. "We're going into Scapa Flow."

Prien then told the rest of the crew, and ordered up a special feast to mark the occasion. It was a strange celebration. The U-boat submerged, and the men sat down to a meal of pork ribs and cabbage. To reduce the risk of detection, the cook, as he served, padded about quietly with his feet wrapped in rags.

Seven and a half hours later, the *U-47,* now on the surface, slipped into Holm Sound, one of three entrances to Scapa Flow. Aerial photographs had indicated to Dönitz that the Kirk Sound entrance on the north of Holm Sound—a slender channel between islands, which was almost completely blocked by three sunken ships—might be negotiated by a daring navigator in a small craft. As midnight neared, Prien stood on his bridge peering into the channel, brightly lit by the flickering aurora. The land closed in on both sides, and the funnels and masts of the sunken ships loomed menacingly above the water ahead. "It is a very eerie sight," Prien recorded in his log. "On land everything is dark, high in the sky are the flickering northern lights, so that the bay, surrounded by high mountains, is directly lit up from above. The blockships lie in the sound, ghostly as the wings in a theater."

To the north, along the coast road of the island off to his right, Prien could see an Orkney Islander cycling homeward, his head lamp glowing weakly in the darkness. Prien had memorized the chart, and he did not bother to refer to it as he guided the U-boat through the passage. He was safely past one of the sunken ships—a two-masted schooner lying in approximately 30 feet of water—when a sudden current turned the U-boat to starboard. The submarine fouled a cable of one of the sunken ships and Prien felt the hull touch bottom. Carefully, delicately, he disengaged the *U-47,* turned slightly to port and then with a difficult, rapid maneuver whisked his boat through the gap. By 12:30 on the morning of October 14, he was inside Scapa Flow.

There another jolting surprise awaited him. As the *U-47* prowled toward the main anchorage with her conning tower hatch open and decks slightly awash, Prien found himself surrounded by a wide expanse of empty water where he had expected to find the Home Fleet. With mounting impatience and anxiety, he edged northward. At last his persistence was rewarded. First he made out the low shapes of destroyers anchored close inshore; then, emerging from the outline of a hill behind them, the masts of two great ships rose against the sky. One was the battleship *Royal Oak* and the other the seaplane carrier *Pegasus* (Prien actually mistook her for the battle cruiser *Repulse).* The U-boat commander gazed with fascination at the *Royal Oak,* and then turned to Endrass. "Here, take a peep at that," he said. "There's another one behind her."

The *U-47* was now 4,000 yards from her quarry, in position for a sensational kill. The four bow torpedo tubes were aimed at the overlapping silhouettes of the two British ships, and Prien gave the firing order. A hiss of air pressure followed, the boat recoiled at the shock of discharge, and the slow, deliberate seconds ticked by as the torpedoes ran.

Three minutes later, with a solid thump, a solitary torpedo exploded harmlessly—evidently against either the *Royal Oak's* bow or her anchor chain. Puzzled and bitterly disappointed, Prien turned his craft away. As he did so he discharged his stern torpedo; it too was wide of the mark.

By now the *U-47's* situation was precarious; surely the whole British fleet was alerted. Prien's instinct was to run for safety. But as he waited apprehensively for the counterattack that must surely come, he began to realize that, astonishingly, no one on board any of the vessels anchored around him suspected his presence even yet. He had no way of knowing it, but both Captain W. G. Benn of the *Royal Oak* and the commander of the 2nd Battle Squadron,

Rear-Admiral H. E. C. Blagrove, who was also on board, had attributed the torpedo explosion to some undetermined internal cause.

Incredibly, Prien had been granted another chance by the British, and this time he proposed to make the most of it. While members of his crew labored to reload the torpedo tubes, he coolly circled for position under the still-flickering northern lights.

Again he gave the order to fire. Again the submariners waited tensely as the torpedoes sped toward their targets.

Suddenly everything happened at once. "There is a loud explosion, roar and rumbling," Prien noted in his log. "Then come columns of water, followed by columns of fire, and splinters fly through the air. The harbor springs to life. Destroyers are lit up, signalling starts on every side, and on land, 200 meters away from me, cars roar along the roads. A battleship has been sunk, a second damaged, and the other three torpedoes have gone to blazes."

Thirteen minutes after the attack, the battered hulk of the *Royal Oak* turned on her side and slid below the surface of Scapa Flow, taking with her 833 officers and men.

The submariners were exultant; but their worst ordeal lay ahead. As Prien turned the *U-47* and sped away toward the escape channel, a clearly visible wake of white water followed behind the U-boat. To port, the land came down close and an automobile speeding along the coast road braked to a halt as its headlights caught the *U-47*'s conning tower. Abruptly the car turned around and shot back the way it had come, leaving Prien certain that he had been located and would soon be attacked.

The tide was sluicing in from the east; even with diesels and electric motors both wide open, the *U-47* crept along at only slightly more than one knot, yet created a high, curling wave to either side. Astern, Scapa Flow was churning with activity, and one of the searching destroyers was drawing near, her searchlight probing ominously. Yard by yard, the *U-47* forced her way toward the narrow gap by which she had entered, at one point barely avoiding a collision with a wooden pier jutting from the island shore.

As the U-boat swung out into Holm Sound, the pursuing destroyer turned and dropped a pattern of depth charges well to the rear, her electronic submarine-tracking device probably having mistaken a sunken wreck for the *U-47*. It was the last close brush. As the U-boat slipped triumphantly back into the North Sea, Prien made one more log note: "The glow from Scapa Flow is still visible. . . ."

For years the German Navy had been the stepchild of the Third Reich, neglected in favor of the Army, pet of ex-Corporal Hitler—and the Luftwaffe, darling of Hermann Göring. Repeatedly Dönitz had argued that the only weapon that could throttle Britain was a large submarine fleet; he had been ignored.

But the Scapa Flow exploit was an eye opener. Two days afterward, on October 16, Grand Admiral Erich Raeder, the commander in chief of the German Navy, distributed a memorandum. "The Führer grants permission for the following measures," it began. There followed a series of war orders; the important one read: "All merchant ships defi-

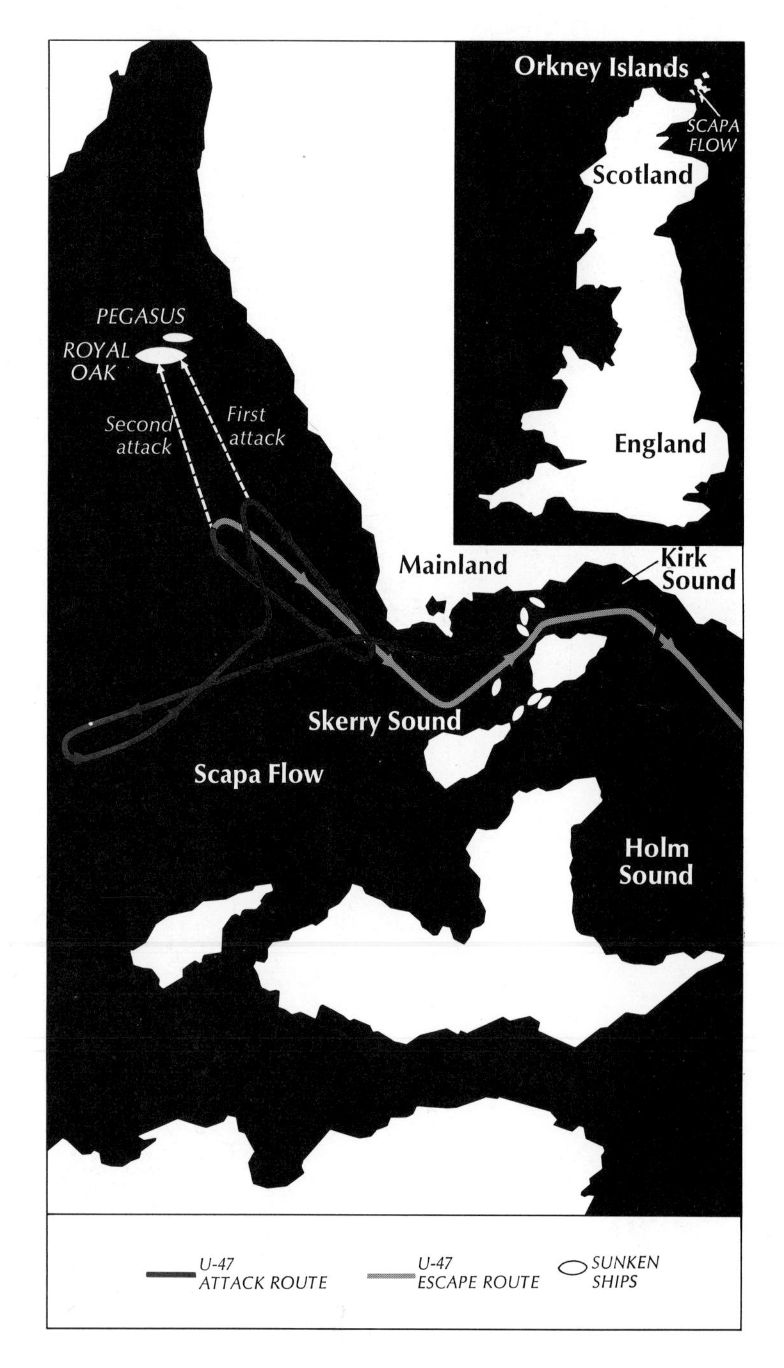

nitely recognized as enemy (British or French) can be torpedoed without warning."

The Raeder order marked the culmination of an increasingly tough German submarine policy. At the beginning of the War, U-boats were still conforming to the Hague Convention, which prohibited attacks without warning on enemy passenger and merchant ships. One British ship—the passenger liner *Athenia*—had been sunk without warning, but the U-boat commander had acted in direct violation of Hitler's orders.

As time passed and it became apparent to Hitler that there would be no quick end to the War, the restrictions against submarine warfare were relaxed. On September 23, the Führer decided that all merchant ships using radios should be halted and sunk or taken captive. The next day, an order forbidding the sinking of French ships was rescinded. On September 30, restrictions against attacks in the North Sea were removed. Two days later, attacks against darkened ships off the coasts of France and Britain were approved, and two days after that the area in which unrestricted attacks were allowed was extended to 170 miles west of Ireland.

Raeder's order after Prien's exploit, removing all remaining restrictions on attacks against Allied merchant ships, turned the U-boats loose against the most important category of enemy ships. Passenger ships still were supposed to be warned. But by the middle of November, even that rule had been dropped.

Two weeks after the *U-47*'s visit to Scapa Flow, Günther Prien and his crew were the guests of their Führer at the Chancellery in Berlin; there Prien was decorated with the coveted *Ritterkreuz*, or Knight's Cross to the Iron Cross.

In the coming months the intensified submarine warfare was to have the gravest consequences for the hard-pressed British. Control of the seas was absolutely essential to Britain. To prosecute its war effort—even to feed its population—the island nation had to import food and raw materials from North and South America and the farthest reaches of its empire in Asia and the Pacific. Mutton and butter from New Zealand, wool from Australia, beef from Argentina, lumber from Canada—all had to come in by freighter. Iron ore was brought in from Africa, rubber from Malaya and grain from Canada, the United States and Argentina. Oil, critical to the running of Britain's war machine, had to be imported over thousands of miles of open sea from the Middle East, the United States, and the Dutch West Indies in highly vulnerable tankers.

To wage any sort of war would prove impossible without an uninterrupted flow into British ports of nearly a million tons of essential materials every week. A fleet of 3,000 merchant ships was required to transport these critical supplies, and almost any day 2,500 of these vessels were at sea. Furthermore, troop reinforcements would be flowing into Britain from across the seas. Both the Canadian and Australian governments were anxious to send men to serve in the European war. As World War II progressed, more and more troops from other parts of the Empire—from South Africa and Rhodesia, New Zealand and India—would be arriving

The daring raid by German submarine U-47 on the British Home Fleet's base at Scapa Flow—located in Scotland's Orkney Islands (inset map at left)—began (red line, large map) when the U-boat entered the protected anchorage of Kirk Sound, and spotted the battleship Royal Oak and the carrier Pegasus. The U-47 scored one inconclusive hit on the Royal Oak, and turned to escape. When no alarm was raised, the submarine circled, and this time sank the battleship. She escaped (gray line) through Kirk Sound. Back in Germany, the U-boat's skipper, Günther Prien (above, right), received a hero's welcome from Commodore Dönitz at the Kriegsmarine base in Wilhelmshaven and was awarded the Knight's Cross. Dönitz was promoted to rear admiral for conceiving the attack.

to play the same role their fathers had played 25 years earlier against the same enemy. Perhaps even the Americans might come in again. All of this meant that steadily growing numbers of ships had to be protected.

The Germans knew, of course, that seaborne commerce was vital to Britain's survival. The admirals of the German Navy had made plans to use battleships and cruisers to sink merchant ships on the high seas. They also planned to sow the waters around Britain with deadly mines, and to employ armed merchantmen disguised to look like innocent freighters to sneak up on unwary captains and blow their ships out of the water. But Dönitz and his staff had always known that their chief hope of blockading Britain lay in the U-boats, which could sink the ships that were bringing supplies and troops across the Atlantic.

In the months that followed, the German subs missed no opportunity. The British, on their part, fought back desperately. They attacked the German surface ships by air and sea, they waged unrelenting warfare against the submarines, and they established their own blockade of the German-occupied European continent. The resulting Battle of the Atlantic was one of the fiercest—and in many ways the most crucial—of all the armed confrontations of World War II. So deadly was it, and so close did the German submarines come to severing Britain's lifeline, that Winston Churchill, Prime Minister through all but a few months of the War, would later recall: "The only thing that ever really frightened me during the war was the U-boat peril."

The Battle of the Atlantic was one that the British at the outset were ill-equipped to fight, even though Britain was the world's foremost sea power.

Britain's unpreparedness stemmed from a variety of misjudgments. First there was the widely held view that the Germans would never again resort to the kind of merciless, unrestricted submarine warfare that had been waged in World War I. There were good reasons for this belief. The London Submarine Protocol of 1936, which the Germans had signed, expressly outlawed the sinking of any unescorted merchant ship without warning. The Protocol also forbade the sinking of any ship without first searching it and discovering contraband aboard. Moreover, the crew of any merchant ship that was attacked had to be assured a safe means of reaching shore, their own lifeboats being deemed insufficient unless land was near. This meant that U-boats would have to surface and expose themselves before making an attack, becoming vulnerable to any ship carrying even light armament and to whatever reinforcements the victim's radio communications could summon.

It was naïve to expect warring nations to honor such legal limitations. In fact, the German Navy's battle instructions contained the following, not unreasonable, order: "Fighting methods will never fail to be employed merely be-

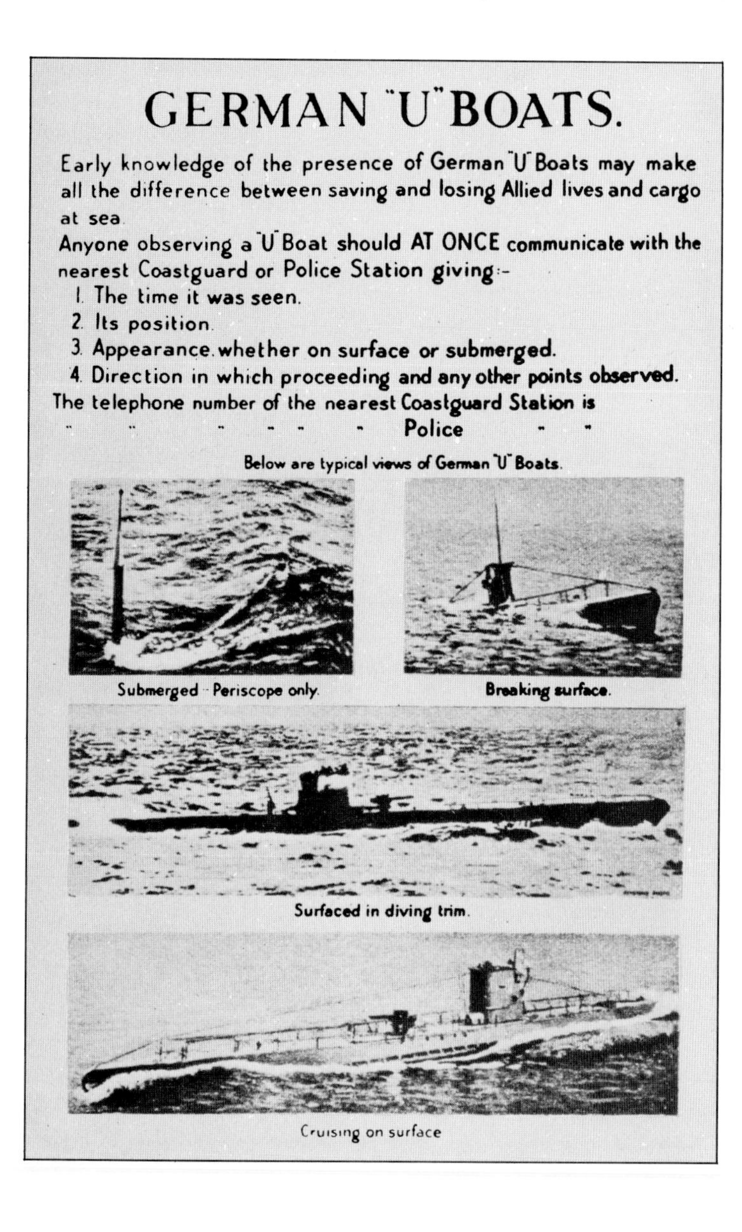
GERMAN "U" BOATS.

Early knowledge of the presence of German "U" Boats may make all the difference between saving and losing Allied lives and cargo at sea.

Anyone observing a "U" Boat should AT ONCE communicate with the nearest Coastguard or Police Station giving:-

1. The time it was seen.
2. Its position.
3. Appearance, whether on surface or submerged.
4. Direction in which proceeding and any other points observed.

The telephone number of the nearest Coastguard Station is

" " " " " " Police " "

Below are typical views of German "U" Boats.

Submerged - Periscope only.

Breaking surface.

Surfaced in diving trim.

Cruising on surface

A poster from a shop in the Orkney Islands exhorts the inhabitants to watch for enemy submarines. Featuring four views of U-boats, the poster lists the facts to be noted and reported to the nearest authorities. In the early months of the War, the Admiralty circulated thousands of these posters for display in public places in the coastal areas of Britain.

cause some international regulations are opposed to them."

Apart from the misplaced faith in treaty obligations and world opinion, there were other reasons within the Admiralty for Britain's lack of preparation for all-out U-boat warfare. The old-line admirals who ran the Navy had been more concerned with Germany's emerging surface fleet than with the potential submarine menace. They envisaged the probability of classic battleship confrontations in which huge battlewagons would try to pound each other into submission, as had occurred during the great World War I Battle of Jutland.

Britain's naval building program in the late 1930s was tailored to that kind of warfare. The five new battleships, six aircraft carriers and 19 heavy cruisers ordered between 1936 and 1939 were better suited for fighting surface fleets than for escorting merchant ships or hunting and killing U-boats.

But as the War got under way, the Admiralty believed that the combined British and French navies were sufficient

New U-boats get final fittings at the Germania Shipyard in Kiel. Krupp, Germany's biggest armament and munitions maker, launched the U-1, the first post-World War I submarine, in secrecy from this yard in 1935. By 1942, the Krupp shipyard was building 20 submarines a year; by the end of the War, it had built 168 of Germany's 1,099 U-boats.

to handle almost any contingency. Although the French Navy was operating chiefly in the western Mediterranean, in the closing months of 1939 it still had units in the Channel ports and the Bay of Biscay. U-boats scored notable successes against shipping during this period, and U-boat strength and efficiency could be expected to grow in the coming months. But so would the antisubmarine potential of the British and the French, and it did not appear to be beyond the capacity of the Allies to contain the threat. As the Admiralty viewed the situation, there was cause to watch the U-boats closely and to develop efficient countermeasures as rapidly as possible, but there was no necessity for undue alarm.

There was still another reason why the Admiralty did not take the submarine threat more seriously; it stemmed from an undue reliance on a weapon developed between the wars. This device led the British to the false conclusion that even if the Germans did resort to all-out U-boat warfare, Allied shipping would be adequately protected.

Toward the end of World War I, a body had been established called the Allied Submarine Detection Investigation Committee. The Committee had produced a range-finding device which, under ideal circumstances, could not only detect a submerged submarine but could also reveal its position. The device, called asdic, from the initials of the Committee (the American version was called sonar), consisted of a transmitter-receiver encased in a metal dome fitted under the hull of the carrying vessel. The transmitter could send out sound impulses on any selected bearing; the receiver would then pick up the impulses when they struck an object and were reflected. The asdic "ping" was a sound that would become familiar to tens of thousands of seamen during the War years, frighteningly so to submariners, who could also hear it. An experienced operator could tell from the pitch of the asdic echo whether a submarine was approaching or moving away. Musicians, with their keen sense of pitch, were particularly good at making this distinction and were much sought after as asdic operators.

The transmitter-receiver was designed so that it could be trained around like a searchlight. When connected to a compass, it would give the direction in which the submarine lay. The time between transmission of the impulse and the return of its echo revealed the range.

As the system was improved and perfected during the War, a group of ships with overlapping asdics could search a wide expanse of the sea, locating all lurking U-boats in the area. But at the beginning of the War, there were serious limitations to asdic's usefulness. The vast majority of the asdic operators were men who had been called up from civilian life and given only a three-month training course before being sent out to sea. Until they acquired extensive experience with the equipment, all echoes were the same: rocks, sunken wrecks, schools of fish, U-boats, even differences in temperature between layers of water. And the number of depth charges carried by any one vessel was not so great that they could be scattered around the ocean every time an ex-civilian who had just finished a training course thought he had located a U-boat.

Even for experienced operators, there were serious technical problems. The sound beam sent out by asdic was conical in shape. The cone pointed away from the transmitting ship, which meant that the area covered by the asdic beams widened with the distance. Within the range of asdic—about 1,500 yards—the farther away a submarine was from the hunter ship, the more likely it was to be spotted. As the submarine and the hunter came closer to each other, the beam narrowed until contact with the sub was lost. U-boat commanders, listening to the ping, quickly

became adept at taking advantage of this gap in contact. The Admiralty was confident, however, that this problem could be overcome, given more time and sufficient training.

But there was another, more serious limitation to asdic. The listening device could be used underwater only. It could not locate submarines on the surface. Aware of the shortcomings of asdic, the canny chief of the German submarine arm, Karl Dönitz, simply ordered his boats to attack at night and from the surface. For the rest of the War, submarines—despite their name—operated for the most part above water, and after dark. They were not only less visible and less audible that way; at top speed, they could travel at 17 to 18 knots on the surface compared with seven to eight knots when submerged. The submarines usually submerged only when danger threatened or a rare daylight attack was to be launched.

The Admiralty was not totally blind to the U-boat threat, of course. The need for escorts to protect merchant convoys had been recognized. Moreover, the urgent necessity for building more antisubmarine vessels was brought home forcefully in April 1939, when Hitler announced his intention to exceed the limits of the 1935 Anglo-German treaty, which stipulated that the two nations would have submarine fleets of the same tonnage.

In response, the Admiralty immediately ordered 56 new escort vessels, the first of the Flower-class corvettes, small, highly maneuverable craft that could be produced quickly and inexpensively in Britain's shipyards.

But the first of these ships would not be ready until the spring of 1940, and it would be a long time after that before there would be enough escort vessels to go around.

When there were, it was preordained by Admiralty policy that they would be improperly used. For British naval planners were ignoring a critical and hard-learned lesson of World War I. In 1917 the Allies had found that the answer to the submarine menace was the convoy. By organizing merchant ships into groups and escorting them with warships, the British had cut their shipping losses by 80 per cent. But in the first year of World War II, a large proportion of the available escort vessels were uselessly employed on search and patrol missions in the ocean's empty spaces. This was wasteful of ships and fuel, and it provided no protection for ships that were traveling at a distance from the patrols. In the early weeks of the War, therefore, many ships were left to travel without escort, and shipping losses were heavy. In the month of September, even before Hitler approved unrestricted submarine attacks, the *Athenia,* the aircraft carrier *Courageous* and 41 merchantmen were sunk.

Eventually, the Admiralty moved to establish an effective convoy system. But it was not until 1943 that Allied ships in the North Atlantic finally got the protection they needed. By that time the battle had been very nearly lost.

At the outset of the War, however, the Germans were not at all sure of their prospects on the Atlantic—despite the high toll of Allied ships (roughly 1.3 per day) during the War's first month. Germany had only 56 U-boats, and 10 of them were not operational at the outbreak of the War. Of the 46 operational submarines, moreover, 24 were small boats most suitable for training and coastal operations—primarily mine laying. And of the 22 oceangoing craft of 500 tons and above, only about a third could be hunting enemy ships at any one time. Experience had established that approximately one third of any submarine force would always be in port for rest, refitting and replenishing while another third would be en route to or from the hunting grounds.

There was an additional problem for the German subs. The long haul from the bases at Hamburg, Wilhelmshaven and Kiel through the North Sea and over the top of the Orkney Islands meant that the time actually spent on patrol in the Atlantic would be greatly shortened. In fact, during the early months of the War, only a handful of German U-boats were operating in the Atlantic at any one time.

When the War broke out in 1939, Raeder, keenly aware of the problems confronting the German Navy, was extremely apprehensive. A veteran of the Battle of Jutland and since 1928 the Navy's highest-ranking officer, he had kept a close eye on the British Navy, and he believed that the German fleet was "in no way very adequately equipped for the great struggle with Great Britain."

Dönitz was equally aware of the weakness of the German Navy, and had been pressing for more submarines. Raeder's chief subordinate, he was a former World War I U-boat commander whose energy and determination were not easily suppressed. Near the end of the earlier war, Dönitz' submarine had been sunk in the Mediterranean. He had

A German contact mine, live with high explosive, rests menacingly on a Dutch North Sea beach in the fall of 1939, after having ripped away from its anchor. Usually submerged in coastal waters, such mines were detonated when a ship bent or broke one of the protruding spikes. Their use by Germany violated an international treaty outlawing them.

been captured and had spent almost 10 months in a British prison camp, and imprisonment had given him an opportunity for contemplation—about submarine warfare in general and offensive tactics in particular.

Following his repatriation, Dönitz remained in the service as one of the 15,000 naval personnel that Germany was allowed under the Versailles Treaty. Because the Treaty limited the German Navy to surface ships, Dönitz was unable to resume his U-boat career. Submarines were seldom far from his mind, however, and while serving with the surface fleet he demonstrated a gift for leadership—an incisive directness coupled with a warmth and sense of personal concern for his men—that was to stand him in good stead later on. In due course he was promoted to command of the modern light cruiser *Emden*. He had just returned to Wilhelmshaven from fleet exercises in July 1935, when Admiral Raeder came aboard his ship with important news. The Anglo-German treaty providing for U-boat parity had been signed. Germany was to have a submarine force again and Dönitz was to command it. The years of training and planning were not to be wasted after all.

Dönitz set about with enthusiasm to rebuild Germany's submarine fleet, and in spite of the years of neglect, he knew that the U-boats and the cadres to run them were readily available to him. Since 1922, German civilians had been quietly designing new submarines for a Dutch firm in The Hague, which was in fact a front for certain German shipyards. Germany's own shipyards had also been secretly busy. Ten days after the 1935 pact became effective, the *U-1*, the first new German submarine, was launched from a heavily guarded shed in the shipyard at Kiel. By the start of the next year, Dönitz had a flotilla of 12 small U-boats.

The new boats were considerably more sophisticated and more menacing than their World War I predecessors. Stronger batteries enabled them to stay underwater for longer periods of time. Their electrically-powered torpedoes—when perfected—left no telltale wakes and were equipped with magnetic firing devices designed to explode under a ship's keel with maximum effect.

To achieve the full impact of his U-boats, Dönitz envisioned a "tonnage war," an all-out campaign designed to sink the maximum enemy tonnage per submarine per day. He believed that the North Atlantic would be the decisive theater of operations and foresaw that when war came—especially if it was against the British—the U-boats would have to carry out their attacks against convoys of merchantmen guarded by naval escorts. A single U-boat in such circumstances might inflict some damage, but a concentration of U-boats, a "wolf pack" as it was to be called, would wreak far greater havoc. There were two problems: to locate the convoys, and to concentrate the U-boats.

The problem of concentration had been made much easier during the interwar years by the improvement in radio communications. Now U-boats on the surface could not only talk to one another; they could communicate with headquarters hundreds of miles away.

A more difficult problem was that of locating the convoys. The most effective method was to spread a picket line of U-boats across the main shipping routes and the approaches to the enemy ports. The first U-boat to sight a convoy could report to headquarters, which would then concentrate submarines for an attack.

This strategy, of course, would require large numbers of U-boats. Dönitz believed that 100 U-boats could do more damage than all the battle cruisers ever built. Given 300 subs, he was confident he could sever England's lifelines.

But Dönitz had to fight for his ideas at every turn. The Navy ran a poor third to the Army and the Luftwaffe in terms of money, matériel and men. Even when Raeder managed to impress Hitler with the Navy's potential, top priority was likely to be given to surface vessels—especially the battleships and pocket battleships, which the Führer thought looked so splendid and which attracted so much attention whenever any of them ventured abroad.

In 1938 a sudden shift in strategy forced the German military services to re-evaluate their roles. Up to that point, planning had been predicated upon a conflict with Poland or France. Now Hitler instructed his military chiefs to add Great Britain to the roster of possible future opponents. The Navy, recognizing its unreadiness for such a war, began a major reappraisal of its overall strategy and its priorities for warship construction.

After months of intense intraservice debate, Raeder presented two alternative plans to Hitler. The less expensive and more quickly achievable plan emphasized tonnage war against British shipping by Dönitz' submarines as well as armed merchantmen and pocket battleships. The other—known as the *Z Plan*—included submarines only as one part of a balanced force of new aircraft carriers, battleships, cruisers and destroyers that could challenge Great Britain's control of the sea.

To the dismay of Dönitz, Hitler opted for the balanced fleet and in January 1939 ordered that top priority be given to its construction. But within nine months, Germany was at war, and the plan became one of the first casualties.

When the Second World War broke out, Dönitz had every available U-boat—46 in all—ready for action in the Atlantic, the North Sea and the Baltic. But he could not keep even a limited number of submarines at sea on a sustained basis, and for a year it was all he could do to replace his U-boats as fast as they were being sunk—a rate of about two submarines per month.

Both the Germans and the British supplemented their battle fleets with another deadly weapon: they sowed their own coasts and the enemy's with thousands of mines, lethal floating explosives that could block ports, tie up convoys and blow up ships. The British, conforming to international agreement, employed only the conventional contact mine, which was moored underwater by cable, and exploded when struck by a ship's hull. The Germans had fewer mines, but some of them were of a more deadly magnetic variety. Planted on the seabed in shallow water, they were set off by the mere proximity of a ship's steel hull.

The British did not find out how to deal with these mines until the summer of 1940, after they had recovered a German mine dropped inadvertently by the Luftwaffe on the mudflats of the Thames estuary. Until then, the magnetic mines defied sweeping, and in November and December of 1939 they sank more ships than Dönitz' submarines.

In the following months, shipping losses—from mines and other causes—mounted rapidly. By the spring of 1940, Britain and its suppliers had lost some 460 merchant ships within a few brief months of warfare. Nevertheless, shipping losses still seemed to be within acceptable limits. Germany's smaller surface fleet appeared incapable of any massive challenge to the Royal Navy. Moreover, an unexpected lull occurred in the U-boat warfare, as Hitler sent his subs to Norway to support the invasion of that country.

But the march of events on land soon radically altered the tempo of the Battle of the Atlantic. On May 10, 1940, the German armies began their great sweep across the Low Countries and Northern France. Holland fell within five days, Belgium in 18 days, and by June 4 most of the British Army had been forced to withdraw from the Continent at Dunkirk. Norway fell on June 8, and by June 17 France was suing for peace.

The British took over six French warships, and destroyed a substantial part of the French fleet at Mers-el-Kebir in Algeria (the bulk of the remaining ships were scuttled by the French themselves at Toulon in 1942). In the meantime, German troops arrived at the Channel ports and on the coast of the Bay of Biscay, and German U-boat crews were soon relaxing in the cafés of Lorient and Nantes. Senior German naval officers—the recently promoted Admiral Dönitz among them—examined the port facilities at Brest and Saint-Nazaire and were soon gazing speculatively out across the bay toward the wide reaches of the Atlantic.

To the British Admiralty, it was clear that the Royal Navy must be prepared to face a new threat: U-boats operating out of the nearby Biscay ports and from Norwegian bases at Bergen and Trondheim. From these bases, U-boats could operate in the Atlantic for greatly lengthened periods of time, receiving more effective guidance and support from squadrons of long-range, land-based planes operating out of Occupied France and Norway. Moreover, the greatly improved situation for the submarines meant that Germany would surely accelerate its U-boat building program.

All of this was happening at a critical time for the Royal Navy. The loss of the French Navy had greatly reduced the number of ships available to combat the U-boats, and had enormously expanded the areas to be covered by the Royal Navy. Moreover, Italy's entry into the conflict in June 1940, plus the need to take over total responsibility for the Mediterranean, imposed an even greater strain.

By now, German surface raiders were presenting a growing threat to Allied shipping. U-boats in increasing numbers were intensifying their efforts with deadly new tactics. The Battle of the Atlantic was beginning its steep climb to a crescendo of violence and destruction that would come close to severing the lifeline to Britain.

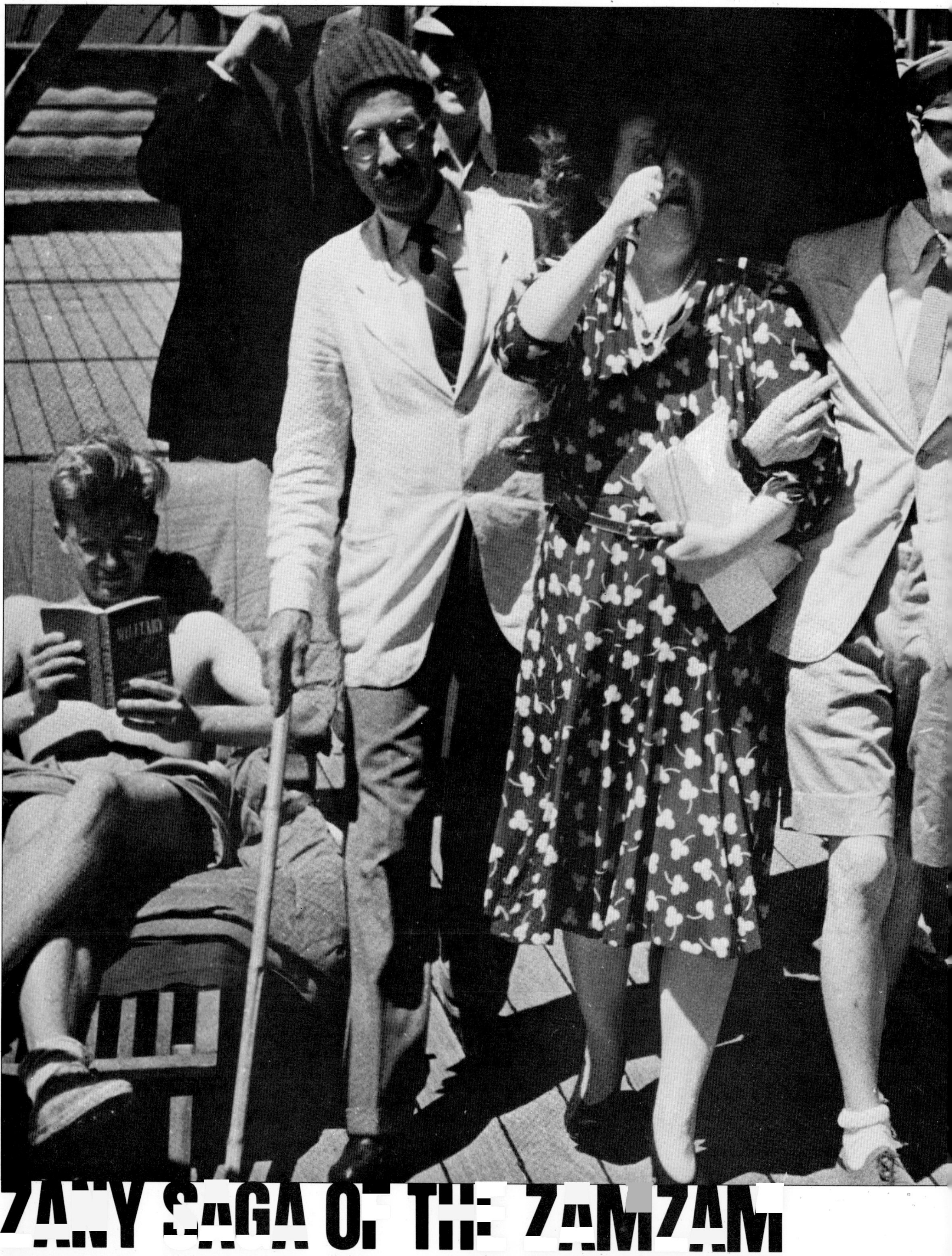

ZANY SAGA OF THE ZAMZAM

guised, the *Atlantis* cruised along the fringes of the route from Cape Town to Freetown, on the prowl for unsuspecting merchant ships traveling alone.

On May 3, the British cargo ship *Scientist* was spotted, bound from Durban, South Africa, to Liverpool with a cargo of grain and chromium. The *Scientist* refused at first to obey Rogge's instructions to stop, and her captain and crew were appalled when the friendly-looking freighter flying the Rising Sun flag suddenly lowered it, hoisted the Nazi colors and opened fire at a range of three miles. The very first salvo bracketed the *Scientist.* It was followed immediately by hits on the stern, the bridge and the radio cabin—but not before the radio operator, though wounded, managed to send the alarm signal QQQ ("I am being attacked by an unidentified enemy ship").

Another salvo from the *Atlantis* landed amidships, and the *Scientist* was doomed. The lifeboats were lowered and the wounded handed down. And the rest of the crew followed and began pulling away from the stricken ship. As twilight thickened, flames broke upward through the decks of the *Scientist* and lighted up the ocean for miles around. The *Atlantis* closed in, finished off the *Scientist* with torpedoes and took aboard the survivors.

This was the beginning of a remarkable odyssey for Captain Rogge and the *Atlantis.* In all, he kept his raider at sea for 20 months of hit-and-run warfare, occasionally rendezvousing with other German ships to share supplies and fuel, and using his radio only rarely to contact headquarters in Germany. To combat monotony on the long cruise, Rogge started a daily newspaper, organized a ship's orchestra, and encouraged songfests and amateur theatricals among the crew. He even devised a system of "leave on board" under which rotating groups of officers and men were relieved of duty for a week or more—except when "Battle Stations" sounded—and were free to enjoy themselves almost like passengers on a holiday excursion.

In those 20 months the *Atlantis* circled the earth, steamed 102,000 miles and captured or sank 22 ships—including the Egyptian ship *Zamzam* with 138 Americans on board *(pages 24-37).* The luck of the *Atlantis* finally ran out in November 1941, off Ascension Island in the South Atlantic. A British cruiser sank her after refusing to believe her signals that she was an innocent British merchantman. But Rogge and most of his crew were rescued by a submarine that happened to be in the area.

Though they were under orders not to engage enemy warships, the disguised raiders usually held their own when battle was forced upon them. The smallest of the lot, the *Thor* —a converted 3,100-ton banana boat—fought two much larger British armed merchant cruisers to a standstill and sank a third. Two other raiders, the *Stier* and the *Kormmoran,* managed, before they went under, to sink the Allied ships that sank them.

Most of the raider captains made prisoners of the crews of the vessels they sank and found ways to transfer them to other ships for delivery to friendly or neutral ports. The exception was Captain Helmuth von Ruckteschell of the raider *Widder,* who became notorious for firing on Allied ships without warning—to prevent them from sending radio signals—and then abandoning the crews in open lifeboats in mid-Atlantic. One such lifeboat drifted for 70 days before it reached an island in the Bahamas. Of its seven original occupants, five had gone mad and jumped into the sea; but two lived to describe their ordeal. Ruckteschell was convicted of war crimes at Nuremberg in 1946 and spent the rest of his life in prison.

Almost all of the 130 ships sunk by the disguised raiders were sailing alone. By late fall of 1940, Admiral Raeder was ready to send his limited force of battleships after bigger game: the Atlantic convoys. In November, the pocket battleship *Admiral Scheer* slipped past Iceland into the northwest Atlantic—the first heavy German ship to be at large since the scuttling of the *Graf Spee* almost a year before.

The *Scheer* quickly found rich pickings: Convoy HX-84, made up of 37 merchant ships protected by a single British armed merchant cruiser, the converted passenger liner *Jervis Bay,* eastward bound from Halifax, Nova Scotia. On sighting the *Scheer,* Captain E. S. F. Fegen of the *Jervis Bay* made one of the heroic decisions of the Atlantic war. Instructing the convoy to scatter, Fegen headed his ship at full speed directly toward the German pocket battleship.

Diverted from the merchantmen, the *Scheer* opened fire with her 11-inch guns at 18,000 yards, well beyond the range of the British ship's six-inchers. The *Jervis Bay* was hit again and again. But still firing those guns that had not been destroyed, she closed to within a mile before being sunk. The engagement had taken only 22 minutes, but it gave the convoy time to scatter.

The *Scheer* raced off into the gathering darkness after the fleeing merchant ships. Of the 37, the Germans found only six; they sank five of these.

The sixth ship—the tanker *San Demetrio*—was to provide a saga of her own. Shelled and set on fire, the *San Demetrio* was abandoned by her crew, who knew that within hours the cargo of gasoline was likely to explode.

But the following day, after surviving a bitter Atlantic gale, one of the lifeboats from the *San Demetrio,* under the command of the second officer, came upon the drifting tanker, which was still on fire but still intact. The survivors decided to go back on board.

When asked later why anybody would want to return to a blazing tanker, Able Seaman Calum MacNeil replied, "She was the only thing we could see in all the wide circle of ocean and she looked good. She might blow up at any time, but that was a quick and painless death compared to this slow freezing and sickness . . . and besides, she was our own ship."

For three days and three nights on sizzling decks and smoldering debris, the crew fought the fires and worked fever-

Oil-soaked crew members of the British destroyer Glowworm, just sunk by the German heavy cruiser Admiral Hipper, wallow on a nearly swamped lifeboat while being hoisted aboard by the raider's crew. The Glowworm was caught alone off the Norwegian coast by the Hipper and four destroyers on April 8, 1940, after parting company with the battle cruiser Renown to search for a sailor who had fallen overboard. Before going down, she managed to ram the Hipper.

ishly to repair the *San Demetrio*'s disabled machinery. At length they got the engines turning again, and the second officer, using a school atlas to navigate, and steering by the blackened stump that was all that remained of the ship's wheel, set a course for Liverpool at a speed of nine knots. On the 15th of November, 10 days after she had been left to sink, the *San Demetrio* made port.

By this time the *Scheer,* aware that the Royal Navy would soon be on her trail, had steamed off for the South Atlantic and the Indian Ocean. Before the *Scheer* returned home five months later, she had sunk 16 ships. More important, the attack on Convoy HX-84—while not a complete success because of Captain Fegen's courageous sacrifice of the *Jervis Bay*—had severely shaken British faith in the existing convoy system. The Admiralty decided that in the future an effort would be made to assign a battleship escort to every major convoy—thus thinning out the Royal Navy's battle squadrons even further.

In January 1941, while the *Scheer* was still at sea, Admiral Raeder also dispatched the *Scharnhorst* and the *Gneisenau* past the British blockade and into the Atlantic. Operating as a team, the two German battle cruisers destroyed 22 ships in two months, including 13 in two days on the Halifax run. The toll might have been higher except for the Germans' reluctance to risk battle and the possible loss of capital ships. On two occasions they turned away from large convoys escorted by single, aged British battleships.

In late March, after successfully evading the British Home Fleet again, the *Scharnhorst* and the *Gneisenau* put into port at Brest in German-occupied France, and the *Scheer* returned to Kiel.

The combined depredations of Germany's heavy warships, disguised raiders and submarines were severely straining Great Britain's resources. Losses in the Atlantic in March 1941 reached 350,000 tons—a new high for the War and a rate that Britain could not long survive. Moreover, Admiral Raeder was now preparing to launch his most ambitious strike of all.

The new battleship *Bismarck,* which had been under construction at Hamburg since 1936, was now ready for sea. Raeder planned to send her into the North Atlantic as the mainstay of a task force powerful enough to attack any convoy, no matter how strong its escort. The *Bismarck* would be joined by the new heavy cruiser *Prinz Eugen* and by the *Scharnhorst* and the *Gneisenau,* which were to sail out from Brest.

The *Bismarck* was Germany's most powerful battleship, yet designed with a grace and elegance that evoked a sense of pride and resurging nationalism in every German who saw her. Though listed at 35,000 tons to comply with the limits of the London Treaty of 1935, the *Bismarck* actually displaced more than 42,000 tons when empty. Measuring 823 feet from her impressively flared bows to her stern and 120 feet wide at the beam, she carried eight 15-inch guns and six aircraft, and was capable of making 30 knots. Most important perhaps, her sides and turrets were protected by 12.6 inches of specially hardened steel.

When the *Bismarck* was launched on St. Valentine's Day, 1939, Adolf Hitler was there to tell a cheering crowd that he hoped her future crew would demonstrate the same unbending determination as the Iron Chancellor for whom she had been named.

After spending more than two years in fitting and shakedown cruises, the *Bismarck* went to war under the command of a cool and experienced gunnery and engineering expert, Captain Ernst Lindemann. The average age of the crew of more than 2,000 was 20. Like the *Bismarck,* most of them were on their first voyage.

Operation *Rheinübung,* or Rhineland Exercise, the code name that Raeder gave his secret plan for the *Bismarck* task force, suffered delays and setbacks. The *Scharnhorst* had developed engine trouble and would have to miss the operation. The *Gneisenau* had been severely damaged in an air attack on Brest. At Churchill's urging, the Royal Air Force had been giving the harbor special attention, and on April 6, 1941, a torpedo bomber piloted by a Canadian, Flying Officer Kenneth Campbell, swept in low to score a hit on the stern of the *Gneisenau.* Seconds later, Campbell's plane was shot to pieces, but the *Gneisenau,* with a smashed propeller shaft and two engine rooms flooded, had been knocked out of action for six months.

No other major ships were available. Admiral Günther Lütjens, whom Raeder had chosen to command Operation *Rheinübung,* now counseled postponement—at least for several months until the powerful new battleship *Tirpitz,* a sister to the *Bismarck,* could be completed. But Raeder was adamant: the *Bismarck* and the new cruiser *Prinz Eugen* would have to go it alone.

Raeder had wanted to launch *Rheinübung* late in April, before the northern nights became too short. But minor damage to the *Prinz Eugen,* caused by a mine, meant further delay. It was not until the evening of May 18, 1941, that the two ships left Gotenhafen, on the Baltic Sea, to attempt the breakout into the Atlantic.

For the first time in the War, German warships had orders to engage the enemy fleet if necessary. Raeder had cleared his plan with Hitler, but knowing the Führer's paranoid fear of losing major ships—"On land I am a hero. At sea, I am a coward"—the admiral did not tell Hitler that the *Bismarck* and the *Prinz Eugen* had sailed until it was already too late to call them back.

The British Admiralty knew about the ships' departure before Hitler did. Coded sighting reports reached London by radio from Sweden and from an alert member of the Resistance in Norway. On May 21, a British reconnaissance plane photographed the *Bismarck* and the *Prinz Eugen* in a fjord just south of Bergen, Norway, where they had paused to take on additional fuel supplies. Two days later another reconnaissance flight indicated that the ships had departed.

By this time, Admiral Sir John Tovey, commander-in-chief of the Home Fleet at Scapa Flow, was moving to intercept the Germans. Tovey sent a squadron made up of the new battleship *Prince of Wales,* the battle cruiser *Hood* and six destroyers, all commanded by Vice-Admiral L. E. Holland, to guard the passages on either side of Iceland. The next day Tovey himself sailed in the battleship *King George V,* in company with the carrier *Victorious,* the battle cruiser *Repulse,* and a screen of destroyers and light cruisers.

Lütjens had circled far to the north under the cover of stormy weather and was picking his way cautiously down the Greenland icepack west of Iceland. There, in the Denmark Strait, the *Bismarck* and the *Prinz Eugen* were discovered in the early evening of May 23 by a patrolling British cruiser, the *Suffolk.*

With her new 13-mile range radar, the *Suffolk,* accompanied by her sister ship, the *Norfolk,* shadowed the larger German ships. Meanwhile, Admiral Holland's squadron raced through the night to confront them, with his flagship, the *Hood,* leading the way.

The "mighty *Hood,*" as the British called her, was the most famous warship afloat. To most of the world, the battle cruiser *was* the British Navy. She had spent the years between the wars proudly showing the Union Jack from Zanzibar to San Francisco, her dignified beauty admired by the millions who saw her and by the hundreds of thousands of visitors—from schoolboys to statesmen—who were invited to tour her decks.

Longer even than the *Bismarck,* at 860 feet, and almost as heavy, the *Hood* had an armament of eight 15-inch guns, comparable to that of her German foe. But by now the *Hood* was getting old. The only notable action she had seen was the shelling of the French fleet at Mers-el-Kebir in North Africa, shortly after the fall of France in 1940.

If the *Hood* was too old for the task ahead, her consort, the battleship *Prince of Wales,* may have been just the opposite. So new was she that gun crews and civilian dock workers were still struggling to make the 14-inch batteries work properly when the ship sailed northwest from Scapa Flow toward Iceland.

Whatever the odds, there was no question that Holland's squadron must find the enemy ships and do everything

An aerial photograph taken from a British Spitfire flying over Norway's Grimstad fjord on May 21, 1941, betrays the powerful new German battleship Bismarck (lower left). The picture was so important that the pilot who took it returned to Scotland, had prints developed there, and then took off for London. When his plane ran short of fuel, he landed about 120 miles away from the city, managed to borrow a car, and drove the rest of the way—through the blackout, at 50 mph.

possible to detain them until Admiral Tovey's force could arrive in support. Shortly after midnight on May 24, Holland signaled "Prepare for Action," and battle ensigns were broken out on both of his great ships.

The anxious hours passed. Aboard the *Prince of Wales* the actor Esmond Knight was serving as a lieutenant. He later wrote: "After minutes of staring at the blank distance, suddenly—and one could scarcely believe one's eyes—there appeared the topmasts of two ships! Again that phrase was shouted by the first man who could find his voice—'Enemy in sight!' "

Knight watched, fascinated, as the *Prince of Wales*'s great turrets swiveled around and the German warships came nearer. "There they were, in deep sharp silhouette on the horizon—*Bismarck* and *Prinz Eugen,* steaming in smokeless line ahead, unperturbed and sinister. 'Ye gods!—what a size!' I heard someone mutter."

The order to fire was flashed at 5:52 a.m. "Almost immediately after there were the great orange flashes and huge clouds of black smoke belching from the for'ard turrets of the *Hood* as she fired her first salvo."

Then it was the *Prince of Wales*'s turn. "Two more moments of unendurable ecstasy, then that pulverising, crashing roar, which for a second seems to knock one senseless—we had opened fire! We were blinded by a dense sheet of flame which rose before us, mixed with clouds of black, bitter-smelling smoke."

The wait was even more unendurable when the German warships, their backs to the icecap, returned the fire. Knight saw "those brilliant flashes and the same jet-black smoke belching from *Bismarck.*" The incoming shells hurtled toward them with a sound like the "approach of an underground train, getting louder and louder and filling the air, suddenly to cease as the first great spouts of water rose just astern of *Hood.*" The thundering shells from the *Bismarck* were punctuated by an "ear-splitting crack" as the *Prinz Eugen*'s high explosive shells, "exploding practically overhead, rained showers of shrapnel onto the decks and into the sea around."

Then, aboard the *Hood,* the worst happened: a shell struck the magazine. As Knight and the others on the *Prince of Wales* watched in horror, "a great spouting explosion issued from the center of the *Hood,* enormous reaching tongues of pale-red flame shot into the air, while dense clouds of whitish-yellow smoke burst upwards, gigantic

Swordfish torpedo bombers on the carrier Victorious are readied for a May 25, 1941, foray against the Bismarck. The canvas-covered biplanes flew more than 100 miles to hit the massive battleship. "It was incredible," said one German officer, "to see such obsolete-looking planes having the nerve to attack a fire-spitting mountain like the Bismarck." Equally remarkable, none of the slow-moving Swordfish were shot down and all of them managed to return safely to the Victorious.

pieces of brightly burning debris being hurled hundreds of feet in the air. I just did not believe what I saw—*Hood* had literally been blown to pieces." Of 1,419 men on the *Hood,* only three survived.

The *Prince of Wales* now became the target for both the *Bismarck* and the *Prinz Eugen.* The British ship's 14-inch guns were working only erratically, and she was hit several times in rapid succession. One shell wrecked her bridge, killing or wounding everyone there except Captain John Leach and the chief signalman (Esmond Knight was blinded). Leach prudently withdrew his ship out of range of the *Bismarck's* guns and joined the *Suffolk* and the *Norfolk* in the task of shadowing the enemy.

Ernst Lindemann, captain of the *Bismarck,* now urged Admiral Lütjens to return to Germany with both his ships. The element of surprise was now gone. The Royal Navy knew the Germans' position, and warships from all over the Atlantic would be converging on them, primed for revenge. Lindemann's advice was not taken, although Lütjens did modify his plans. He detached the *Prinz Eugen* to hunt for enemy merchant vessels while the *Bismarck* made for the French port of Saint-Nazaire and repairs. The *Bismarck* had been hit by only two English shells, but one of them had ruptured a fuel tank. She was trailing oil and, until the tank could be repaired in dry dock, her range would be reduced. If he could not shake off the *Suffolk,* the *Norfolk* and the *Prince of Wales,* Lütjens planned a nasty surprise for them. He radioed Berlin to ask that a line of six U-boats be formed between himself and the French coast, over which he would draw his pursuers.

During the night that followed, the *Bismarck's* antiaircraft guns fended off an attack by torpedo-carrying Swordfish planes from the carrier *Victorious.* Then for six hours, the *Suffolk's* radar lost track of the *Bismarck.* But Admiral Lütjens, not realizing that his pursuers had lost contact, chose this time to send a long radio message to Berlin describing the engagement in the Denmark Strait. The message took more than 30 minutes to transmit. That was more than enough time for British direction-finding radio sets to zero in on the *Bismarck* again. Then the British navigators erroneously plotted their quarry 200 miles north of her actual position. The *Bismarck* lengthened her lead while the British force steamed in the wrong direction, wasting time and precious fuel.

Incredibly, the German radio traffic continued, and British cryptanalysts were able to decode enough of it to determine that Lütjens had the *Bismarck* on course for Brest. On the scent once more, Tovey swung his force to the southeast. Most of his destroyers and cruisers, by now low on fuel, had to head for home. The damaged *Prince of Wales* was also forced to give up the chase. But the battleship *Rodney,* slower than the *Bismarck,* but with nine powerful 16-inch guns, had been diverted from convoy duty to join the chase. Still more British ships were steaming up from the south to try to cut off the *Bismarck.* Among them were the carrier *Ark Royal,* the battle cruiser *Renown* and the cruiser *Sheffield,* all from the Royal Navy's Force H, stationed at Gibraltar. The net was closing in, if the *Bismarck* could only somehow be slowed down.

At midmorning on May 26 a long-range Catalina flying boat, dispatched from Northern Ireland, sighted the *Bismarck* some 700 miles from the coast of France. That afternoon the *Ark Royal* launched 15 of her Swordfish biplanes armed with torpedoes with magnetic exploders. But by mistake they attacked the cruiser *Sheffield,* which had gone ahead to scout. Only some wild maneuvering by the *Sheffield* in the stormy seas, and the fact that most of the magnetic exploders on the torpedoes were faulty and exploded prematurely, prevented the British pilots from sinking one of their own ships.

Before darkness fell, the *Ark Royal's* planes had enough time to make one more attack. It would be the last chance to get the *Bismarck* before the battleship reached friendly cover. This time, as the planes took off in gale-driven rain, they carried torpedoes that were equipped with the older, more reliable contact exploders.

The *Bismarck* blazed away at the incoming Swordfish with 56 antiaircraft guns. But the flimsy canvas covering that made the old-fashioned planes appear to be so fragile actually helped them to survive. Shell splinters tore the canvas to shreds but did not cause the fatal shattering that might have occurred with a metal fuselage.

Two torpedoes struck the *Bismarck.* One did no damage, but the other smashed into the steering engine room. That hit was to prove disastrous to the great battleship. The

Bismarck had been in a hard turn to port when the torpedo struck; now both her rudders were jammed at a 15-degree angle. Every combination of her engines served only to bring her bow plunging into the wind, toward the northwest—and the approaching Home Fleet.

Aboard the *Bismarck* a night of despair followed. A flotilla of five fresh destroyers appeared to harass the stricken giant. Admiral Lütjens offered to reward the Iron Cross on the spot to any volunteer who could blast free the jammed rudders in the flooded engine steering room. But every effort failed. Even a message from the Führer: "The whole of Germany is with you," did little to revive the flagging spirits of the *Bismarck's* exhausted crew.

Morning brought more squalling rain, and the British battleships *King George V* and *Rodney* were closing in rapidly from the northwest, supported by the heavy cruisers *Norfolk* to the north and *Dorsetshire* to the south. At 8:47 a.m. the *Rodney* opened fire from 12 miles away, followed immediately by the *King George V*. The *Bismarck* returned their fire, but she was barely maneuverable.

The *Rodney's* third salvo destroyed one of the *Bismarck's* forward turrets. Splinters swept the bridge. The *Norfolk* and the *Dorsetshire* joined the fight. Shell after shell smashed into the *Bismarck's* superstructure. Her fire control machinery was demolished. The *King George V* and the *Rodney* closed to four miles, then to two miles—point-blank range. Observers saw shell after shell from the British ships strike home. By 10 a.m. the *Bismarck* was still afloat and under way, but her guns were silent.

At 10:15 a.m., Lieut. Commander Gerhard Junack, the *Bismarck's* chief turbine engineer, was told that the ship was sinking. With difficulty, he made his way topside. "There was no electric light," he wrote later, "only the red glow from numerous fires; smoke fumes billowed everywhere; crushed doors and hatches littered the deck, and men were running here and there, apparently aimlessly: it seemed highly unlikely that one would survive."

Assuming command of the crew milling about on the deck, Junack told the men "to make their last preparations and then gave a few simple orders—stay together in the water, keep calm, don't give up hope, and be careful when interrogated by the enemy. After a triple *'Sieg Heil!,'* I ordered 'abandon ship.' Hardly were we free of the ship when it keeled over to port, rolling the deck-rail under and bringing the bilge-keel out of the water. A pause—then *Bismarck* turned keel-up, slowly, the bows rose in the air, and, stern first, *Bismarck* slid down to the bottom."

Of the more than 2,000 officers and men who had sailed from Gotenhafen nine days earlier, only 110 were rescued. Neither Admiral Lütjens nor Captain Lindemann was among these survivors.

Thus ended Operation *Rheinübung*, and with it the major effort of Germany's surface navy in the Battle of the Atlantic. Within a month the Royal Navy—again aided by information from the cryptanalysts who were decoding German maritime wireless traffic—located and destroyed half a dozen supply ships that were vital to sustained German operations in the Atlantic. A few disguised merchant raiders remained at large until the end of 1943, but for the most part they limited their clandestine work to the Indian and Pacific oceans.

The *Prinz Eugen* eluded the British hunters and reached Brest four days after the *Bismarck* went down. But the French port was within easy reach of the increasingly dangerous RAF. In February 1942, the *Prinz Eugen*, the *Scharnhorst* and the *Gneisenau*—screened by no fewer than 60 smaller escort ships and 250 aircraft—succeeded in a surprise daylight dash up the English Channel and under the cliffs of Dover to the relative safety offered by German ports on the North Sea.

By this time, the *Bismarck's* sister battleship, the *Tirpitz*, had joined the German fleet. But her effectiveness was limited. Hitler, who was still haunted by the loss of the *Bismarck*, had decreed that all of his remaining major ships must "avoid any unnecessary risks"; none could sail without first obtaining his express approval. By now also, Germany's supply of the high-quality fuel oil that was needed to drive a battleship's turbines was running low enough to necessitate careful rationing.

Admiral Raeder stationed the *Tirpitz* in northern Norway as the centerpiece of a force that for two years would help to make the "Murmansk Run" a murderous gauntlet for Allied convoys trying to bring supplies to Russia. But never again would the big ships venture into the Atlantic to sink Allied vessels.

That was left to the submarines.

SUICIDE OF A MARAUDER

With a Nazi ensign whipping at the stern, the new pocket battleship Graf Spee gets ready to join an international naval review at Spithead, England, in 1937.

THE GRAF SPEE'S LAST DAYS

In the *Graf Spee's* marauding days, crewmen watch from the pocket battleship's deck as another of the raider's merchant victims goes down.

One of the most dramatic episodes of the early days of the Battle of the Atlantic, the attack by three British ships on the powerful pocket battleship *Graf Spee,* gave a few days of unaccustomed prominence and diplomatic intrigue to the neutral port of Montevideo, Uruguay. The damaged warship—with 57 wounded and 37 dead on board—had sought refuge there, but found herself instead in a trap. British vessels blocked her exit and the Uruguayans refused to extend the 24-hour layover permitted by international law beyond a 72-hour grace period granted ships needing repairs.

This suited the British, for at the end of the 96 hours the *Graf Spee* would either have to limp out of port with her repairs incomplete and engage their warships, or remain at anchor, subject to international law that would require her to be seized and her crew interned. Then the British discovered that she was not so damaged as they had believed. Anxiously, they cast about for a scheme to prevent her from escaping before the 96 hours were up.

Since international law forbade a warship of a belligerent nation to leave a neutral port for a day after the departure of a merchant ship of the opposing side, British diplomats rushed a note to the Uruguayan government stating that one of their cargo vessels would be sailing in a few hours. The government accepted the note, but did no more than send a small tug to deter the warship if she too set sail.

It was plain to the chief of British intelligence that something drastic had to be done. But time was running out. He had a brainstorm: "Let us lead the Germans to believe that we have heavy reinforcements arriving." The trick would be to leak the information to the Germans, via a fake telephone call to the British ambassador—whose line was known to be tapped by German intelligence—and a planted story in a newspaper in neighboring Argentina.

But the captain of the *Graf Spee,* Hans Langsdorff ("a high-class person," in the words of Winston Churchill), knew there was no escape. The steps he took to save his honor and keep his ship from being seized form the gripping finale to the story of the *Graf Spee.*

At a Montevideo cemetery, Captain Hans Langsdorff uses a naval, not Nazi, salute in final tribute to members of his crew who were killed in action.

Part of a crowd of a quarter of a million jams the quays and harbor docks at Montevideo on Sunday, the Graf Spee's last day in port. The spectators expected to be witnesses of a great sea battle, but the battle never came off.

Smoke and flames envelop the once-mighty Graf Spee, scuttled by her captain in the River Plate. The fire burned for four days, and the structure was so hot that for two more days the hulk could not be boarded.

Waving to friendly crowds ashore, crewmen from the Graf Spee depart for Buenos Aires on an Argentine tugboat that made its way up the shallow River Plate. Most of the seamen were interned in Argentina, but some managed later to escape and get back to Germany.

The crew of the scuttled Graf Spee holds its final muster with Captain Hans Langsdorff (inside circle, hands on hips) in a courtyard of the Naval Arsenal in Buenos Aires. The captain spoke briefly to his crew, saluted them and then went off to his quarters in the arsenal. There he committed suicide.

Stiff-armed Nazi salutes honor Captain Langsdorff as his funeral cortege

accompanies his coffin to its grave in Buenos Aires' Chacarita Cemetery. A British merchant captain also attended, sent by the officers Langsdorff had captured.

Jubilant crewmen on the British cruiser Exeter celebrate their triumph over the Graf Spee. The Exeter bore the brunt of the fighting as the Graf Spee was chased into Montevideo. Afterward the British warship, badly damaged, withdrew to the Falkland Islands for repairs.

Through London's Admiralty Arch and past throngs of cheering civilians march the crews of three British cruisers—the Ajax, the Achilles and the Exeter—

that helped to bring about the Graf Spee's end. Their victory in the Battle of the River Plate boosted British morale in the dark early months of the War.

and members of her crew are violently shaken by the explosion of a depth charge. The submarine's commander was one of Germany's top U-boat aces

Celebrating a successful patrol, a submarine crew joins in singing beer hall songs with accordion accompaniment and plenty of lager. Once their torpedoes

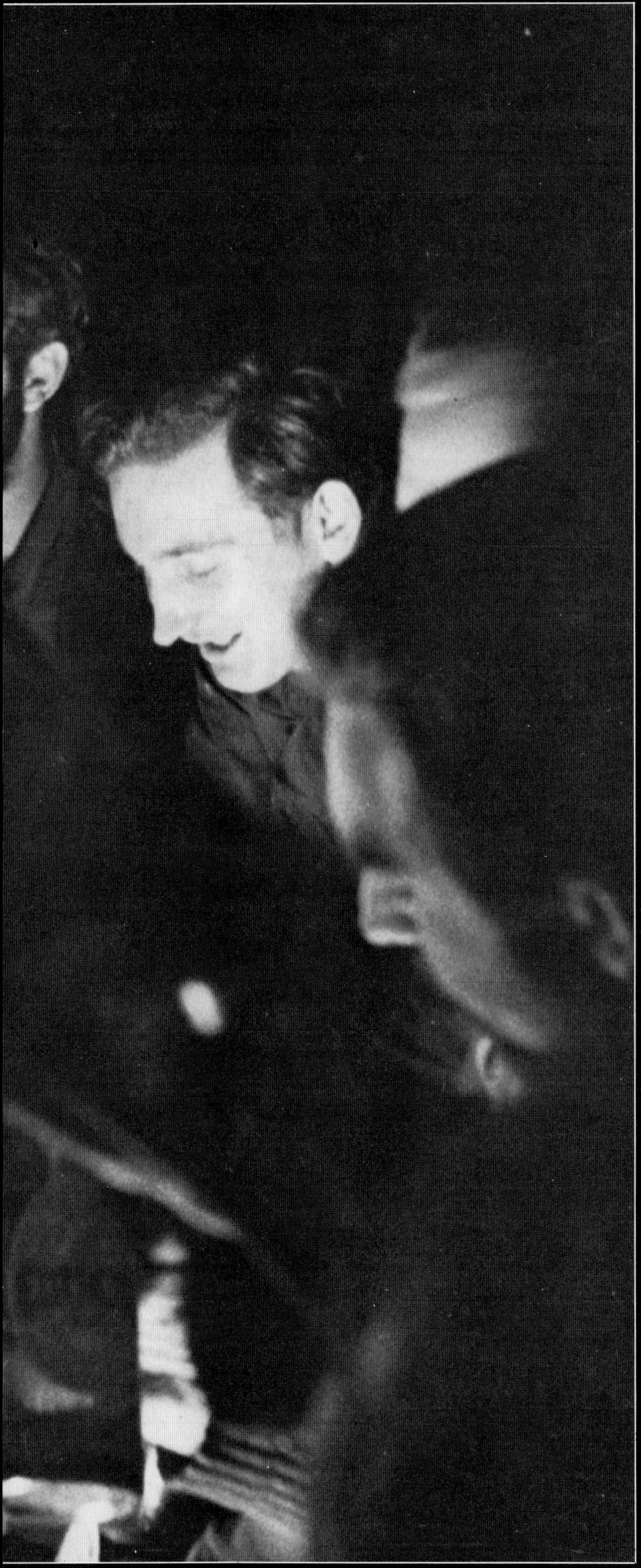

were used up, the U-boat men could expect a week or more of shore leave.

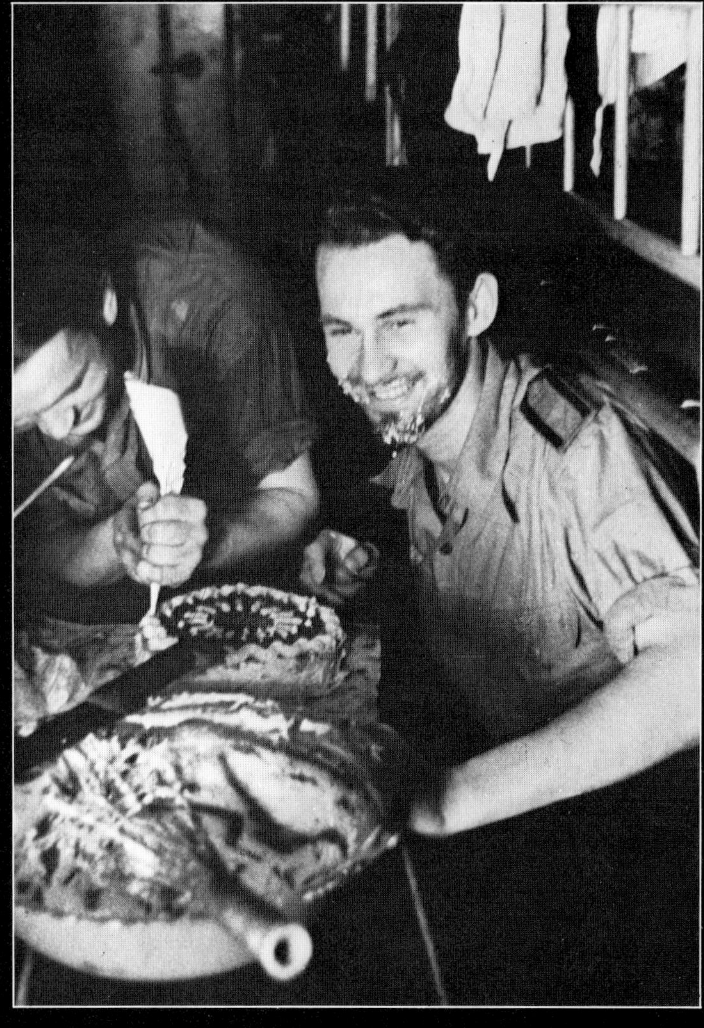

In a lull during a patrol in the Atlantic, submariners take time out to decorate a cake and sample its icing. The cake was baked in the sub's cramped galley for a celebration of an officer's birthday.

Bound for home, a U-boat crew paints pennants with the tonnage of Allied ships they sank during the patrol. The flags were flown from the conning tower as the sub entered port, to cheers from waiting comrades.

THE SINKING OF A U-BOAT

Exploding depth charges produce a mountainous geyser from the deep as the U.S. Coast Guard cutter Spencer attacks the German submarine U-175.

A BRIEF RISE BEFORE THE FINAL PLUNGE

The terror that U-boats spread was matched by the terror that the men on the U-boats faced. For being a U-boat captain or crew member was one of World War II's most hazardous occupations. Statistics tell the grim story. Germany lost 28,542 of its 41,300 submariners, and 753 of its 863 operational U-boats. The sinking of one of those boats by Allied vessels is recorded in the dramatic pictures on these pages, from the moment the depth charges were dropped until the crew of the fatally damaged U-boat surrendered and was marched off to a prisoner-of-war camp.

The episode began when Captain Gerhardt Muntz, while searching from his conning tower for Allied ships in the North Atlantic 600 miles west of England, spotted an approaching convoy. At the same time, Muntz's submarine, the *U-175*, was herself seen by the U.S. Coast Guard cutter *Spencer* in the vanguard of the convoy. Hastily, the *U-175* dived, and for a short time successfully evaded detection. But trailing the *Spencer* in 11 parallel columns were the 19 tankers and 38 freighters of Convoy HX-233, an irresistible target. Muntz decided to chance an attack. It was a fateful decision. As the *U-175* eased up from the ocean depths, the *Spencer* passed right over her, and the cutter's sonar detection device picked up the sub.

Commander Harold S. Berdine, aboard the *Spencer*, ordered an immediate depth-charge barrage: 11 of the lethal drums, set to explode underwater at 50 and 100 feet. Then, anxious to neutralize the sub before the convoy arrived, Berdine released 11 more depth charges. The furious assault worked: the *U-175*'s air pumps and diving controls were damaged, and Muntz had no choice but to bring his crippled submarine to the surface.

As the *U-175*'s conning tower rose into view a mile and a half behind the cutter, the convoy ships and the *Spencer*'s sister cutter, the *Duane,* opened fire. It was all over in moments. Captain Muntz and six of his crew died on the *U-175*'s deck. The remaining crew members jumped overboard; while they were still bobbing in the seas, the *U-175* sank to the bottom.

A submariner calls out for assistance from the Spencer moments after the U-175 sank. Calm, warm (54° F.) seas made rescue work less hazardous.

The badly damaged U-175 surfaces and is immediately caught in a fusillade of artillery and machine-gun fire as the cutter Spencer closes in for the kill.

The U-175 goes down stern first as officers and men from the Spencer, who had boarded the sub for a quick inspection, watch from a lifeboat nearby.

Saved from drowning, a submariner from the U-175 grabs a boarding net on the cutter Duane. Dangling near his cheek is his life-jacket mouthpiece.

A dazed U-boat survivor is led off by two of the Spencer's crewmen. Commander Berdine of the cutter later reported some of the survivors as "hysterical" during the rescue operation.

Resentful German submariners are ordered to peel off their clothing while being searched aboard the Duane. The captured men told the cutter's officers that the first salvo of depth charges from the Spencer cracked the sub's hull, jammed her forward steering mechanism and broke her air pump system.

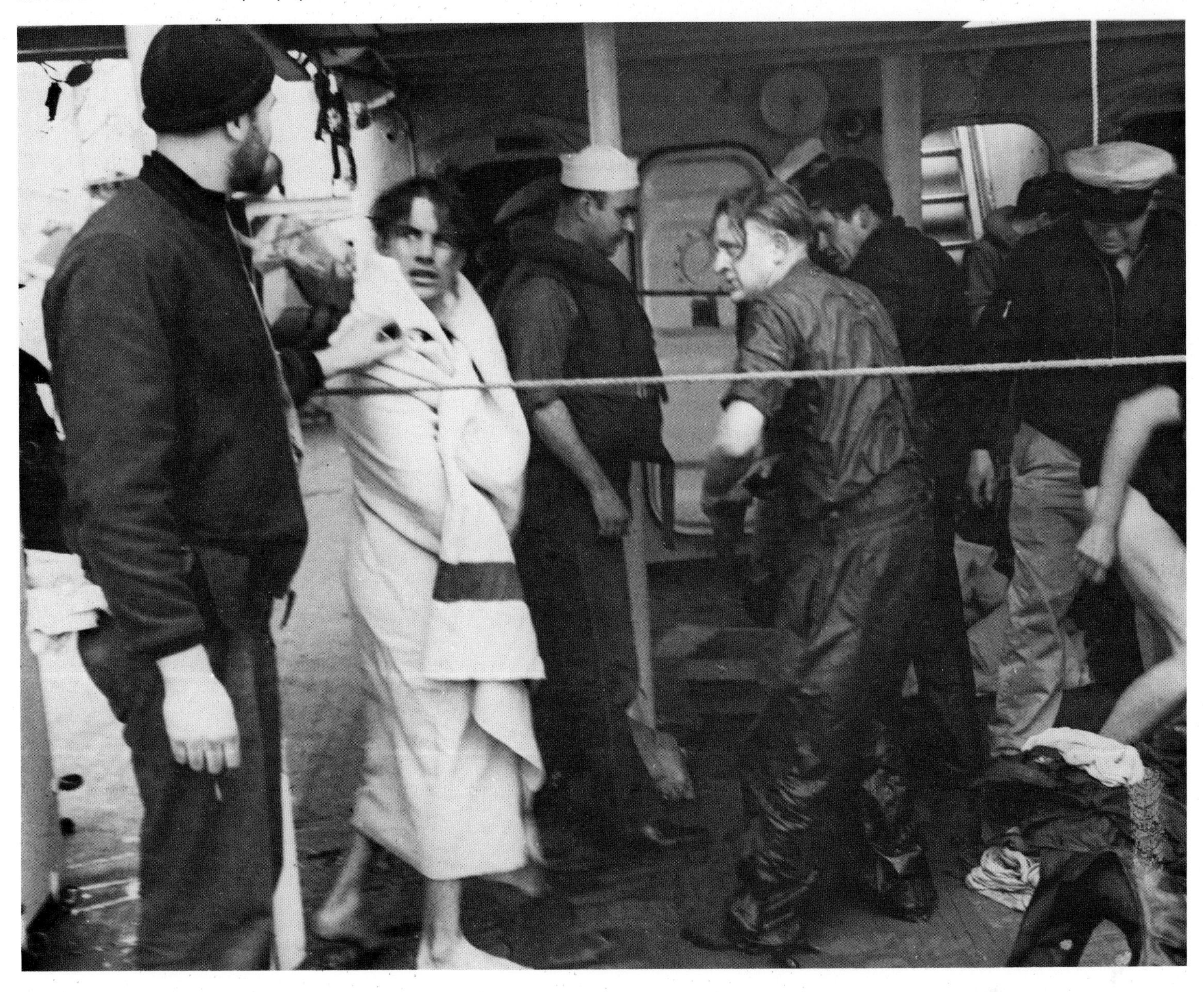

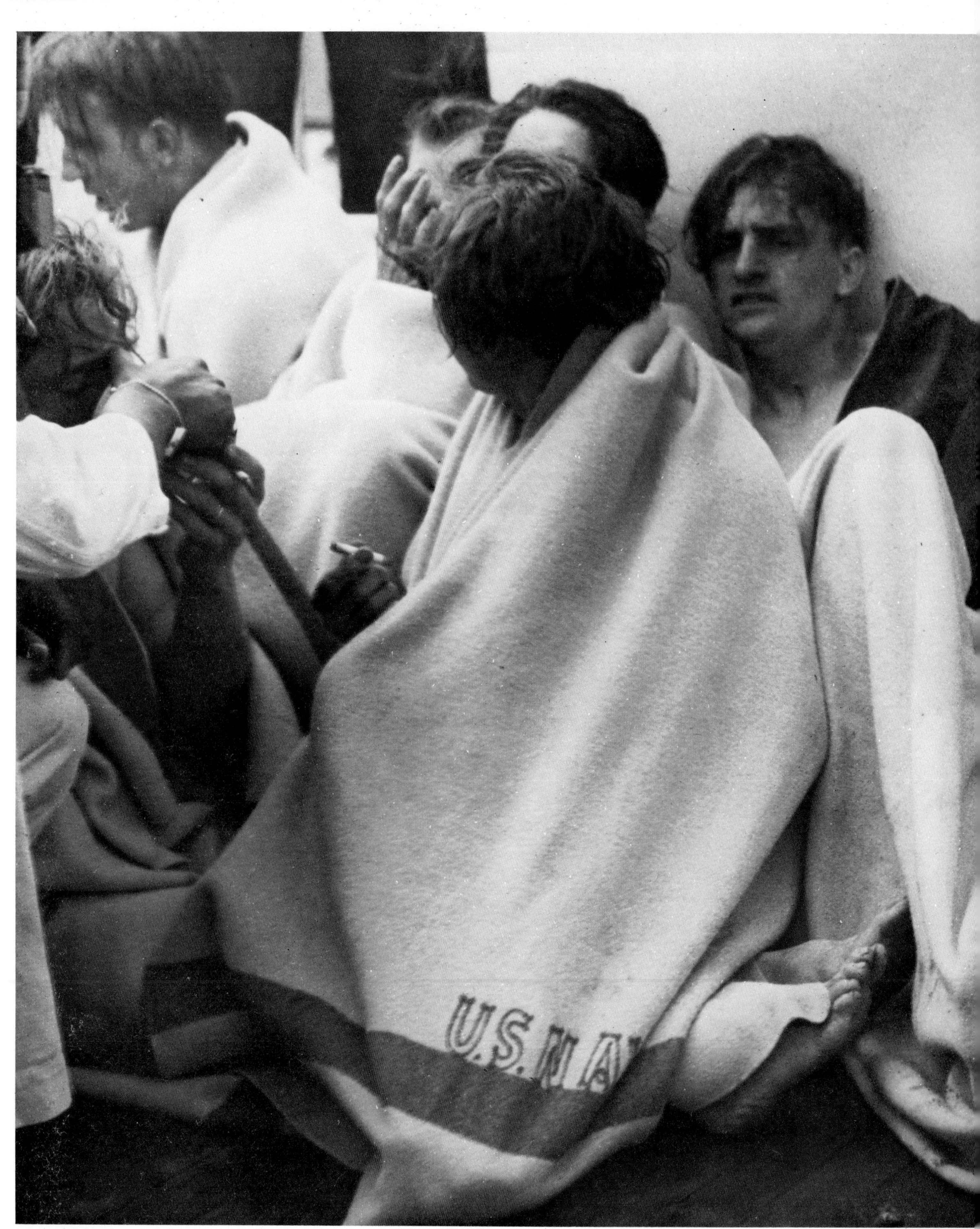

Swathed in blankets and showing stress, the U-175's survivors huddle on the Spencer's quarterdeck. Taken below, they were dressed in borrowed denims and fed

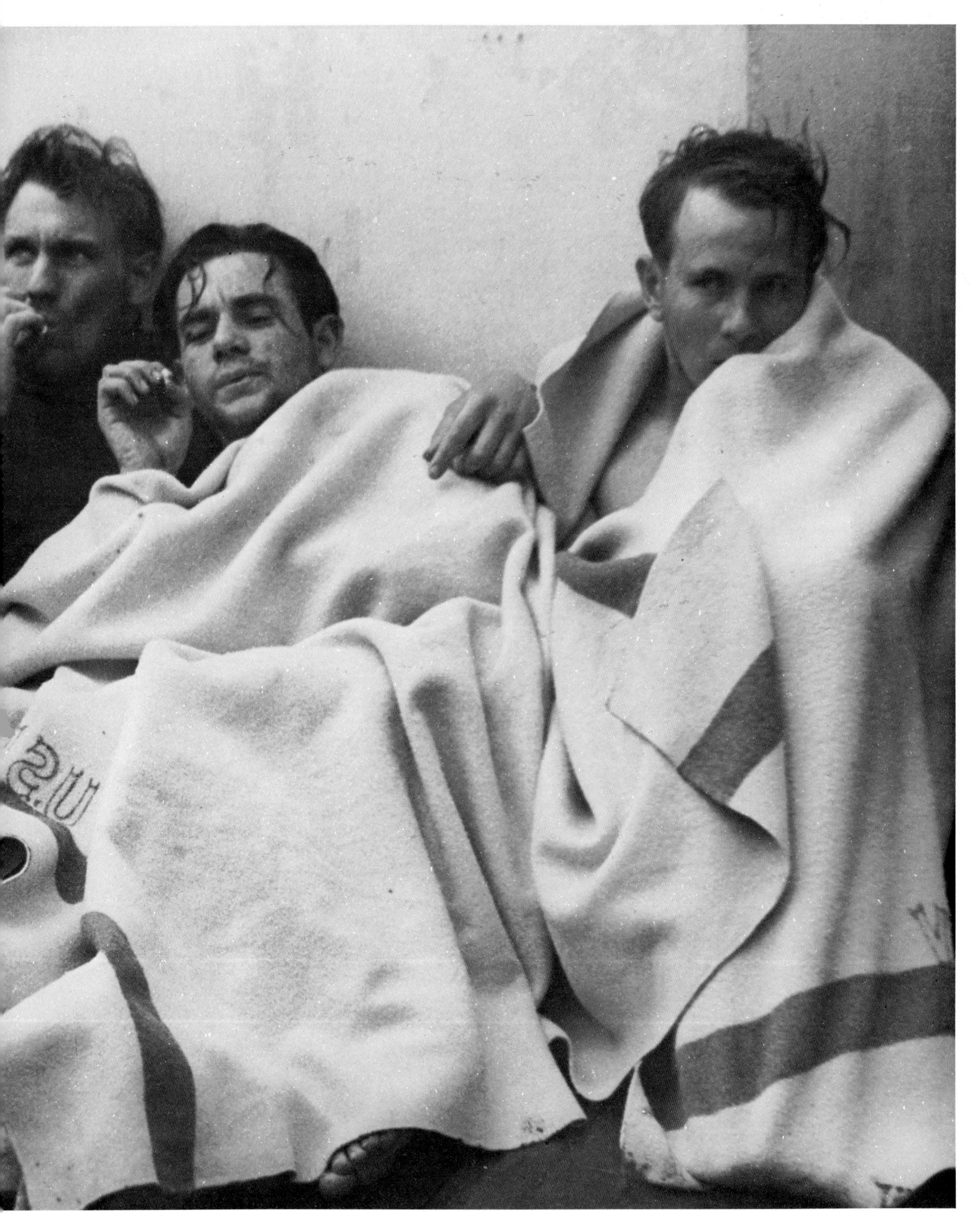

a meal of corned beef and potatoes. The Spencer rescued 19 members of the U-175's crew. Twenty-two more German sailors were saved by the cutter Duane.

Triumphant members of the Spencer's crew line the rail in front of a Popeye cartoon painted on the funnel to celebrate their victory over the U-175. It was the second kill for the ship.

Commander Harold S. Berdine (front right) and his fellow officers celebrate the sinking of the German submarine at a victory dinner in the flag-decorated wardroom of the Spencer.

British Marines march off the German prisoners of war from the U-175 at Gourock, an Allied naval base at the mouth of the River Clyde in Scotland. From there they were taken by transport to a prisoner-of-war camp. The Spencer and Duane are docked behind the prisoners.

Some yachting gentlemen put to sea
The anguish of the Bluebell's crew
An ocean lit up like Piccadilly Circus
Best defense against the U-boats
Nightmares of the merchantmen
The fate of ships that strayed
Working the kinks out of the convoy system
A British crash course in survival
A timely American gift
Tough vessels named for flowers
The U-boats' telltale chattering
End of the line for three undersea aces

VITAL ARMADAS

For the weekend sailors who so gallantly responded to the advertisement in the London *Times* suggesting that "gentlemen with yachting experience" apply for commissions in the Royal Navy Volunteer Reserve, there was a sudden and rude awakening when they found themselves aboard the escort vessels that accompanied the first convoys. In place of white sails were guns and depth charges; in place of beautiful girls were tired, grim-featured and often acid-tongued commanding officers, who were trying to carry out a difficult job that was made even more difficult by inadequate equipment, poor supplies, and a lack of planning and coordination between ships with similar responsibilities. It was a long time before things got better; before that, they got much worse.

The hard-bitten merchant captains who sailed in the first convoys had a similar experience. The convoys were badly organized, makeshift collections of 30 to 45 freighters and tankers that were attempting the novel experience of sailing 3,500 miles together in close formation. A large number of the ships were so decrepit and unseaworthy that only the urgent demands of wartime made it at all possible to justify their use.

The conditions of the ships and the inexperience of their crew members made the duty of the escort vessels an especially onerous one: they had to accompany these motley armadas, shepherd them through dangerous waters, protect them from submarine attack and bring them safely to port. The task was awesome; yet the very outcome of the War depended upon its being carried out successfully. It would have been a challenge to the most grizzled of seamen, but at the beginning of the War, the Royal Navy had had no other choice than to man the escort vessels with any able-bodied recruits it could find—weekend sailors and even those who were without any previous seagoing experience at all. The adventures of a little corvette called the *Bluebell* were typical.

Commander Robert Evan Sherwood first took the *Bluebell* to sea in the summer of 1940. It quickly became apparent to him that "only three or four of the crew of 52 were capable of any real action of any kind at all." Of his three officers, two were Canadians. "They were fine chaps, but they had had very little training. One was a lawyer and the other was in the leather business. One of them was very pale but went green when he was seasick, which sometimes lasted for two days. Once I was in my cabin and the ship was not quite doing what she should be doing, so I asked: 'How is your head?' I wanted to know where we were going, for on a ship 'head' means 'course.' He answered, 'Much better, thank you, sir.' "

Sherwood counted himself fortunate to have gained his experience on small ships, because corvettes, "though fine ships, are not the easiest." The *Bluebell* seemed to be always wallowing, always fighting the sea. She "would do everything except turn over," Sherwood noted. "In bad weather the cook couldn't control the galley to give everyone proper food—not that there was much desire to eat. It is one thing to be able to do something on land or in good conditions and another to be able to do it in bad conditions when you are seasick. Then you have to be able to do it in your sleep."

In October, the *Bluebell* got its first big taste of battle as one of the escort ships accompanying Convoy SC-7, the ill-fated convoy that was first spotted by Heinrich Bleichrodt in the *U-48* on October 16. The convoy consisted of 35 elderly, lumbering vessels that were on their way to Great Britain from Nova Scotia.

Typically, the escort for SC-7 had been flung together in a hurry. In addition to the *Bluebell,* there were two sloops. The commanders of these vessels had never met before, and there was almost no coordination among them, although they had been forewarned by the Admiralty that there were U-boats in the area in which they were traveling. A predawn attack by Bleichrodt was their first intimation that trouble was at hand: two ships were sunk. One of the escort vessels fruitlessly depth-charged the suspected point of attack and the convoy pushed on. Then, the following night, the U-boat pack struck en masse. Suddenly there was a tremendous flash—another one of the SC-7's ships had been hit. "I was on the bridge," recalled Sherwood; "it was around 8:15 p.m. I went in towards the convoy to see if I could get any information." He searched the area where he thought the explosion had taken place, but could determine nothing, in part because the escort ships had established no organized procedure for communicating information to one another during an attack. "I had never seen the *Fowey,* one of the sloops, before and she had never seen me. We each did what we thought best at that particular moment."

The wolf-pack onslaught created total havoc. "Suddenly it was 'bang, bang, bang!' and the place was lit up like Piccadilly Circus." A total of 16 ships went down; one was sunk when she stopped to pick up survivors. At the height of the disaster, Sherwood again moved in to see what was happening. None of the escort vessels had ever experienced a pack attack before, and no one could understand how a single U-boat could inflict so much damage. To add to the confusion, someone suddenly opened fire on the *Bluebell.* Whether it was a submarine or a merchant ship, Sherwood did not wait to see. He put another ship between the *Bluebell* and the line of fire, knowing that in the heat of battle a corvette could be mistaken for a submarine by a merchantman.

The confusion quickly turned into a nightmare. "We were fumbling around in the dark," Sherwood reported. "There were survivors all over the place. The attack went on until one or two in the morning. I never saw an escort that night. And I didn't drop a single depth charge and I don't think anyone else did."

In fact, the only useful service that the escort vessels performed after the wolf pack had struck was to pick up survivors. Sherwood alone took on board 308 men.

The following night a similar calamity befell the 49 ships constituting Convoy HX-79 and its escort. Faster than SC-7, HX-79 also had much more formidable protection. Two destroyers, a minesweeper, four new corvettes and three asdic-fitted trawlers formed a protective screen around the convoy. Yet HX-79 lost 12 ships without being able to inflict the slightest damage in return—once again as the result of a wolf-pack attack.

The experience of Lieut. Commander G. T. Cooper, in charge of one of the destroyers, the *Sturdy,* sounds much like Sherwood's. Cooper and his crew had had only one previous turn at escort work in submarine areas, and that had proved to be uneventful. "I had no details of this convoy, nor did I know the nature of the escort and I had never met any of the Commanding Officers of the other ships. No plan of action in the event of attack had therefore been discussed between us."

When the attack developed, each ship took individual action as fresh emergencies arose. The flanks of the convoy went unprotected for long periods of time, while the escort vessels violated one of the first principles of effective convoy discipline by running off from the ships to follow up elusive contacts with the enemy or to pick up survivors. As the night wore on, the convoy and its escorts found themselves strung out along an ever-thinning line. All told, HX-79 lost almost one quarter of its total force, and this despite its traveling with an escort that was numerically strong enough to provide it with ample protection.

In just two nights, 28 merchant ships had been destroyed by the wolf packs, and every one of the attacking U-boats had escaped unscathed.

So ineffectual did escorts appear in the face of wolf-pack attack that men at all levels of command began to wonder whether it made any sense to bunch ships together to form huge targets for the enemy to strike at will.

The problem was twofold: a lack of discipline and a chronic shortage of escort craft. The shortage had been accentuated by shipping losses suffered in the spring and summer of 1940 in the fall of Norway and France. The subsequent establishment of German submarine bases in France made it impossible for British ships to use their own Channel ports—primarily Southampton, Plymouth and Portsmouth—and effectively closed off access to Great Britain from the southwest. In the entire area of what the British called the Western Approaches, the only access remaining from the west was the route around Northern Ireland, through the North Channel and across the Irish Sea to Britain's west-coast ports, Liverpool and Glasgow.

Since even the doubters could find no substitute for the convoy system, the convoys went on. Assembling one and shepherding it across the sea involved a host of enormously complex problems. The difficulties began to assert themselves from the moment the ships came together at their initial rendezvous point—more often than not, outside the Nova Scotia ports of Halifax or Sydney if eastbound, and outside Liverpool or Glasgow if westbound. Freighters large and small joined with tankers old and new, perhaps a passenger ship or two, sometimes a merchantman converted for heavy cargo such as tanks, trucks or landing craft.

Unequal in size, these ships differed as well in their maneuverability, their mechanical condition, their speed, their capacity for maintaining their positions, their signaling and other equipment, the caliber of their crews, even the ability of the men to make out orders shouted from the bridge—which might be manned by Dutchmen or Poles, Norwegians or Danes, Belgians or French Canadians. And even when English was the common language aboard ship, a Scotsman did not always find it easy to understand his mate from Southampton, and vice versa.

Once a convoy was under way, it would form into a wide rectangle of eight to 12 short columns, with 1,000 yards between columns and from 400 to 600 yards between the stern of each ship and the bow of the one following *(pages 126-127)*. A 40-ship convoy (30 to 45 merchant ships constituted the average aggregation for the first three years of the War) would be arranged in eight columns five ships deep, covering an area almost four miles across by about two miles deep. Only four or five escorts could be spared by the Navy from duty elsewhere to guard the perimeter. And in charge of this tiny force would be the command ship, usually an old World War I destroyer, placed ahead of the formation, or at a point from which—depending on weather conditions or perhaps the position of the moon—an attack might come.

Difficult as it was to keep the armada operating as a unit, there was an additional complication in the matter of command. The escort commander was responsible not only for the conduct of the escort ships, but for the entire convoy. On his shoulders fell the job of directing changes in course and issuing whatever other instructions were necessary for the safety of all the ships. The convoy commodore, from his flagship among the merchant ships, was responsible for maintaining the internal discipline of the convoy proper, in terms of navigation and holding to position.

Unfortunately, there were times when the duties and responsibilities of escort commander and convoy commodore overlapped. This caused a certain awkwardness, especially when the escort commander, usually a commander or lieutenant-commander in the Royal Navy or the Royal Canadian Navy, was considerably junior to the convoy commodore, who was likely to be a retired rear-admiral or vice-admiral with the acting rank of commodore, Royal Naval Reserve. It took more than a little mutual tact and courtesy for an admiral to accept orders given to him by a youthful lieutenant-commander. Whatever friction developed was generally minor and short-lived. Both officers understood the necessity for cooperation.

Once the armada was in formation, it had to be guided round the clock by the escorts across a sea that could be glassy one day, turbulent the next. The ships had to keep station, that is, they had to stay in their proper positions in the convoy, and make as little smoke as possible in order to avoid attracting a sub. When laden with their precious cargoes, they wallowed sluggishly into the danger areas of the eastern leg of the voyage near the northwest Irish coast, where the U-boats waited. When empty and riding high on the return voyage, the convoy ships might have to butt their way into howling gales in order to reach the refuge of North American ports.

Through it all, the escorts acted as watchdogs, chivying the laggards into place, scurrying about with instructions to close up, ease out, make less smoke, or tighten the blackout at night. There was another problem: occasionally a merchantman disobeyed sailing instructions and left oil trails, dumped garbage and pumped bilges in daylight—telltale signs for the enemy to spot.

Even when all was going well, there was the continual shield for the escorts to provide: the constant weaving back and forth across the front of the formation with asdic directed ahead to pick up submerged foe lying in wait; out and in again along each flank, watching for attackers sneaking in as dusk fell; the constant patrolling astern, always on guard against the surfaced U-boat, whose commander knew quite well that only one escort ship, or two at most, could be spared to crisscross the wide tail of the convoy—and that four to six miles was a wide stretch for just one or two escorts to cover.

At any moment, there might come a warning of danger ahead: a signal flashed to indicate a sighting. And the whole plodding mass of shipping had to be turned in concert to dodge the threat, often making so sudden and sharp a curve that the ships on the inside of the turn were crowded dangerously close together while those on the outside became so widely separated as to risk losing contact with one another. Now the commanders of the escort ships needed all their skill, their foresight and their patience—and all the speed that could be coaxed from their overworked engines. Inside the convoy, the commodore worried about the dangers of collision as the ships turned simultaneously to their new course away from the threatening U-boat. And when it was all done and the convoy was safely on its new course with the danger point well astern, the whole maneuver had to be repeated in the reverse direction to get the convoy back on its original course.

Often the U-boats would not be detected in time for either evasive or offensive action to be taken. Sometimes, as at night, the danger was not apparent until the enemy had

Bobbing like corks and every bit as seaworthy, corvettes like the one at left above were the ideal convoy escorts, inexpensively produced and able to survive and maneuver in the worst kind of weather. But the 1,010-ton vessels were notoriously uncomfortable. Because of their broad beams and rounded bottoms, they rolled viciously, tossing sailors out of their bunks and making even the hardiest skippers queasy.

unison upon a prearranged signal during a U-boat attack.

The combined firing could light up the sea for miles around; if there were U-boats lurking in the area, they were often starkly revealed. Snowflakes were two-edged weapons, however, because they also made clearer targets of the ships that fired them. Still, it was kill or be killed, and if snowflakes gave the escorts the chance to fire the first shots or release their depth charges on target, they were worth the risk.

One elementary change that greatly enhanced the survival rate of ships in convoys came not from any breakthrough or improvement in military hardware, but from a careful analysis of sinkings. Operational Research, a little-noted backroom unit of the Admiralty, concluded that the number of vessels lost in any convoy depended upon the number of attacking submarines and the size of the escort, and was not in any way related to the number of ships there were in the convoy.

For example, if a wolf pack attacked a convoy of 20 ships and sank 10, it did not follow that the same wolf pack attacking a convoy of 70 ships would sink 35. It would, in fact, probably sink no more than 10; a much greater proportion of a large convoy would get through safely.

As a result of this study, the British sharply increased the size of a typical convoy from about 30 ships to 50, 60 and sometimes even more. This also meant that more escort vessels could be allotted to each convoy and that there would be fewer convoys at sea at any one time for the submarines to attack.

Larger convoys did mean a larger area for the escorts to defend—a seeming disadvantage. But basic geometry demonstrated that two small convoys had in fact more exposed perimeter to be protected than did one convoy twice the size. As luck would have it, this basic discovery came at a time when the number of escort vessels available for convoy duty was rising.

The twin problems of providing enough escort vessels for the convoys and of extending adequate protection all the way across the Atlantic were greatly eased by the Canadian contribution to the Allied effort. When the War began, the Royal Canadian Navy was little more than a token force: six destroyers, five minesweepers and some 3,000 officers and men. Yet by 1941, Canada had taken full responsibility for guarding the convoys on the western leg of the Atlantic run. It could do so because of an ambitious ship-building and training program launched by Prime Minister Mackenzie King; before the War was over, Canada would send almost 400 ships and 90,000 Canadians to sea.

The potency of air power as a weapon against submarines had been proved in World War I, but like so many lessons of that war it had to be learned all over again in the Second World War. When the British organized a convoy system in 1917, they reduced their shipping losses by 80 per cent. And when aircraft—even the primitive planes of that era—were added to the convoy escorts to spot and attack lurking U-boats, the losses became almost negligible. Out of all the ships that were protected by air cover, only five were sunk by the Kaiser's U-boats.

In World War II, it soon became evident to the Allies that the approach of one of their planes, even one that carried no effective weapons, had an electrifying effect on a surfaced U-boat. The submarine usually dived as fast as she could for the safety of deep water. And the dive cost her opportunities. The submerged U-boat found it much harder to detect approaching ships. And if she were tracking a convoy, she was much more likely to lose contact underwater, because her speed was greatly reduced. If the plane's sighting report brought escort ships to the scene quickly enough, they could use their asdic to seek out the submarine and attack her.

In the years between wars, the British had done little to prepare their air arm for a war against submarines. Aside from the fact that the U-boat menace was not considered a major threat by the military planners, there were relatively few pilots available who had been trained for sub spotting in any case. Before the end of the First World War, the Royal Naval Air Service had been absorbed into the RAF, and in the intervening years few pilots had been trained in naval aviation of any kind.

With the establishment of the Fleet Air Arm in 1937, the Royal Navy regained control of its own air wing, but only so far as carrier planes were concerned. The RAF's land-based Coastal Command was still responsible for all other maritime aircraft, and the Navy remained the orphan of British aviation. The planes assigned to the Navy generally were

Clothed against flashback, a British sailor in a foul-weather coat helps ready a depth charge for firing aboard the corvette Rhododendron. Ship's officers (background) search the water for evidence of the success of previous firings. The explosive-filled cans were rolled off the stern and fired off the sides. The resulting diamond-shaped patterns generally consisted of 14 charges, enough to encompass a submarine.

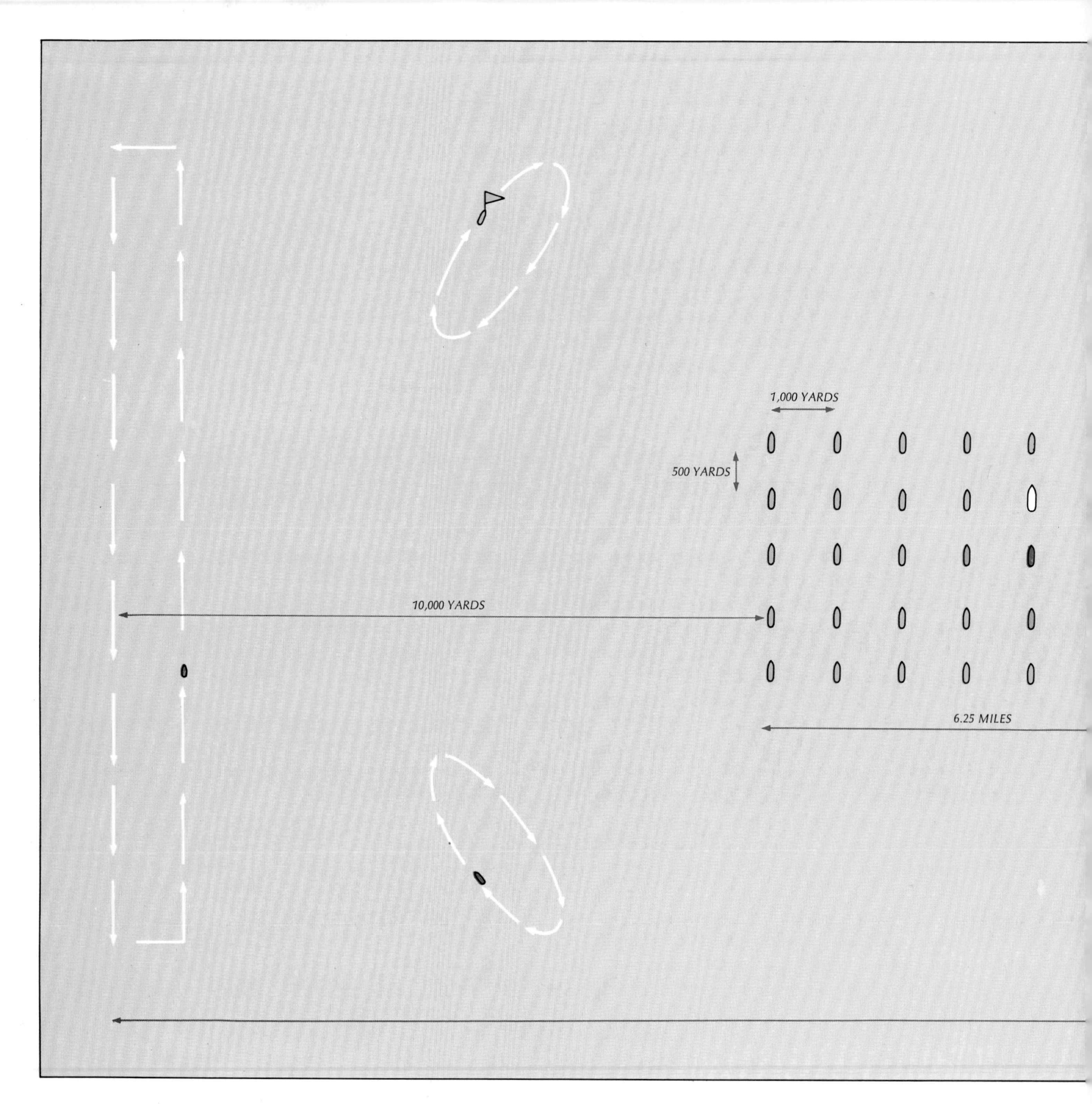

CARGO SHIPS: RAW MATERIALS; TANKS, PLANES AND OTHER EQUIPMENT; AMMUNITION
TANKERS
TROOP SHIPS
DESTROYER ESCORTS
CORVETTES
CONVOY ESCORT COMMANDER
CONVOY COMMODORE

DIAGRAM FOR A WINNING COMBINATION

When the War was over, Admiral Karl Dönitz wrote: "The German submarine campaign was wrecked by the introduction of the convoy system." Diagramed above is a typical 1942 convoy, whose formation made it difficult for U-boats to score a kill, even at night when they could operate on the surface.

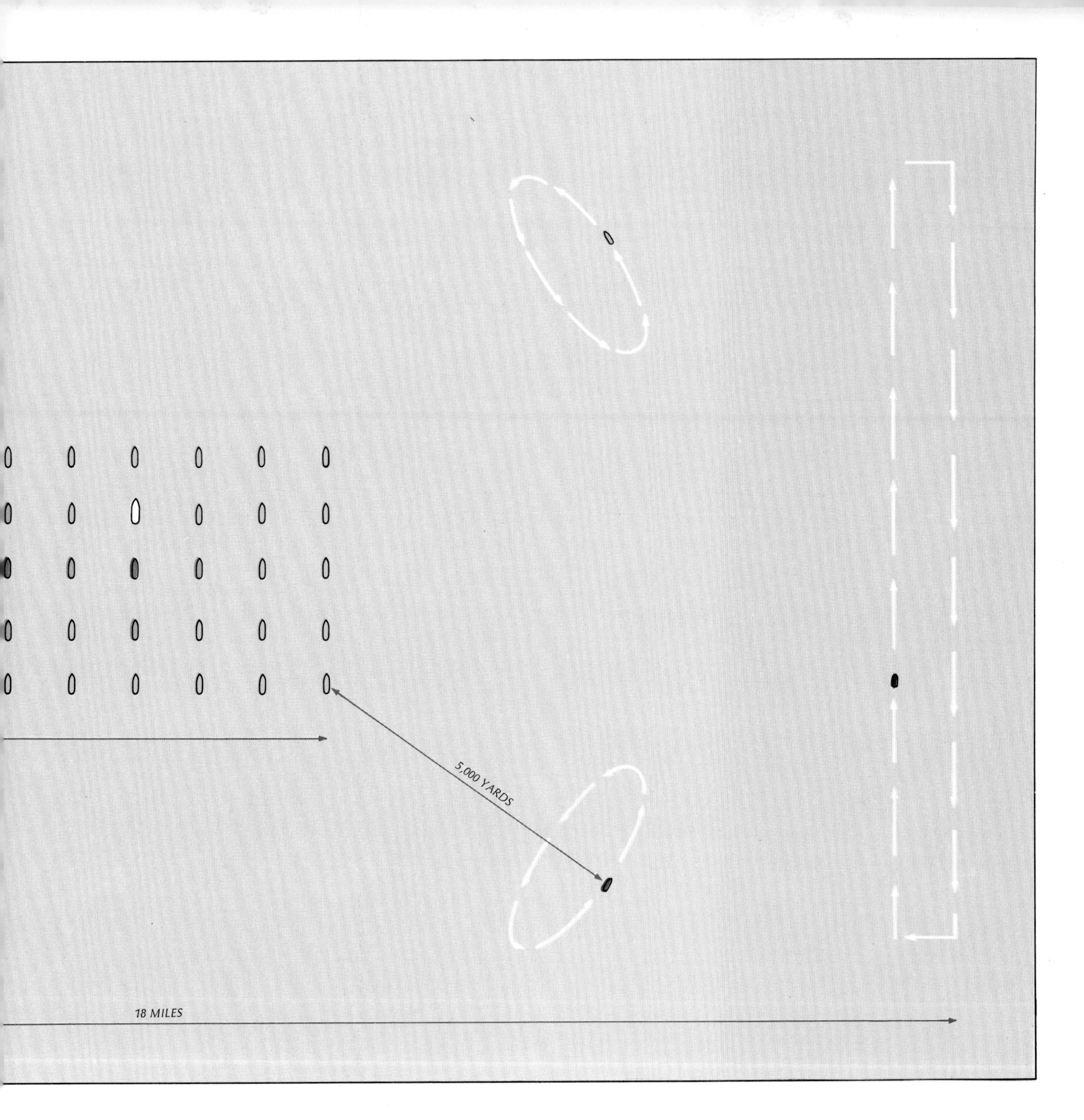

Because the merchant ships presented the biggest target from bow to stern, the convoy's vessels were deployed only five deep, thereby minimizing the number exposed to flank attack. Oil tankers, troop transports, ammunition ships and vessels loaded with tanks, guns and other vital war matériel were placed inside the formation. (Ammunition ships were never positioned next to one another—or to oil tankers—for fear a torpedo hit might set off a chain reaction of explosions or fires.) Around the convoy's core were cargo ships carrying expendable raw materials (cotton, wheat, ore). Ships were spread over an area 18 miles wide and spaced carefully to provide maximum safety while maintaining close contact with one another.

In this typical formation the convoy is accompanied by two destroyer escorts and four corvettes. The destroyers patrol in elliptical patterns to prevent attacks from the front, while two corvettes guard the rear. The other corvettes patrol its flanks.

The convoy commodore, who was responsible for the merchant vessels and saw to it that they maintained their positions, rode front and center. The escort commander also rode up front, but on the convoy's portside. Under U-boat attack, the escort commander took charge of the entire convoy, issuing orders to the convoy commodore, even when outranked.

RAF castoffs, or aircraft originally designed for land use that had to be modified drastically for carrier duty and were so vulnerable and tricky to fly that their pilots referred to them as "flying coffins."

When the War began, RAF Coastal Command was in sole charge of protecting shipping and patrolling the waters off the British Isles from the air. But Coastal Command also was neglected. At the start of the War, it had only 170 multi-engine seaplanes and conventional land-based planes available for antisubmarine duty, most of them obsolete, with limited range and combat effectiveness.

Moreover, Coastal Command's plight could not improve in those early days. First priority in the building of new aircraft and the training of men to fly them went to RAF Fighter Command, which used its resources heroically in the air battles over Britain in 1940. After that, the inauguration of the strategic bombing campaign against the German homeland led to a massive build-up of RAF Bomber Command. A few naval voices argued that the resources devoted to the bombing of German cities could be used more profitably in the battle against submarines. The voices went unheeded, and after more than a year of war, Coastal Command possessed barely 50 more planes than it had when the fighting started.

In addition to the shortage of planes and trained men, Coastal Command suffered severely from poorly conceived tactics in the same way that the Navy did. Instead of being deployed just above or reasonably close to the convoys —and thus discouraging the U-boats by their presence— the airplanes were more frequently dispatched independently on wide sweeps of the empty ocean. It was the old "search and patrol" doctrine all over again, and the results of such missions were just as unrewarding from the air as they had been on the sea.

When a plane did happen across a surfaced submarine, the pilot had no effective weapons with which to attack her. At the outbreak of war, planes sent out on antisubmarine duty were supplied with small bombs, but they were not equipped with bombsights. The bombs had to be dropped from very low altitudes, and pilots had to rely on their eyes alone to aim them.

The hazards of this system were dramatically illustrated on the 14th of September, 1939, when two dive bombers from the British carrier *Ark Royal* spotted a German U-boat that was cruising on the surface. The submarine, under the direction of Lieut. Commander Fritz-Julius Lemp, was homeward-bound after having been responsible for the sinking of the British passenger liner *Athenia*. The pilots dived as low as they dared, let go their bombs and began to climb away—only to discover that their bombs had skipped over the surface of the ocean and bounced up into the air underneath the planes. The fuses had been activated by the impact of the bounce, and the bombs exploded, spraying

the planes with shrapnel and forcing the pilots to ditch in the Atlantic. Lieut. Commander Lemp picked up the two men and took them back to Germany aboard his submarine.

The incident of the bouncing bombs was repeated more than once until the British perfected an effective airborne depth charge. It was an adaptation of the Navy's depth charge, fitted with fins and a rounded nose to give it more stable flight, and set not to explode until it reached a certain depth underwater.

But depth charges dropped from the air had to explode close to a U-boat if they were to inflict any serious damage on her steel hull. This was not easy when the target was moving and could suddenly disappear beneath the surface in a crash dive. Experience born of missed opportunities gradually taught the airmen that their only real chance for a kill was to concentrate their firepower by dropping a number of depth charges all at once while the submarine was close beneath the surface—25 feet was about the limit of effectiveness.

As 1941 got under way, the planners were beginning to recognize the importance of air power in the antisubmarine campaign. Coastal Command was given more and better aircraft; included were some 30 American-built Catalina flying boats, which could cruise for 17 to 25 hours at a time. With new equipment and growing experience, the pilots became increasingly battle-wise. One simple trick involved painting the undersides of planes white instead of black, which made them more difficult to see against the sky.

In the spring, operational control of Coastal Command was turned over to the Admiralty. This assured the Navy of top-priority air support, while leaving the officers and men of Coastal Command in the RAF, where they traditionally belonged. With summer, air coverage in the Atlantic was improved. A squadron of Lockheed Hudsons, another squadron of old seaplanes and a third of long-range fighters began flying air cover out of Iceland, thus reducing by 400 miles the part of the mid-ocean convoy routes that was beyond the reach of protective aircraft.

The effectiveness of airplanes as antisubmarine weapons was severely limited in the early part of the War by their inability to spot their targets at night. Early attempts to equip Coastal Command planes with radar in 1940 had failed. But scientists had persevered and by 1941 many planes were being fitted with cumbersome sets that required mounting large antennae on either side of a plane's rear fuselage, two smaller forward-looking antennae underneath the wings and reflectors built on posts on top of the fuselage to receive the return signals. Inside the plane a member of the crew—usually the navigator or radio operator—had the additional duty of monitoring the radar screen. On one type of plane, the Whitley, used by Coastal Command, the new equipment was installed in such a way that to use it the operator had to sit on the seat of the plane's toilet, midway along the cold and dank tunnel of the cabin. It was not popular duty.

Early airborne radar—known as ASV, for air to surface vessel—had another limitation: it lost contact when the target came too close. At a range of about one mile, the blip that indicated the position of the submarine disappeared from the screen. On a dark night, a U-boat could escape. But the gap was eventually bridged by adding a powerful searchlight to each plane. The technical problems of developing such a light were overcome by the ingenuity of an RAF officer named Humphrey de Verde Leigh. Squadron Leader Leigh had been a pilot in World War I but had been relegated to a desk job at Coastal Command headquarters because of his age. Leigh heard about the radar-gap dilemma almost by accident and, being a determined fellow, set about to invent a light that could be mounted under an aircraft. He came up with one that was powered by a small

Three of Britain's most effective aerial weapons in the Battle of the Atlantic were the Sunderland flying boat (far left), which carried bombs and depth charges and bristled with machine guns, and was dubbed the "flying porcupine" by the Germans; the ancient-looking Swordfish biplane (center), which laid mines, dropped flares and attacked submarines and surface raiders with torpedoes; and the catapult-equipped merchant ship, which carried a Hurricane fighter that strafed U-boats and ships and attacked German aircraft, but could not return to deck once launched.

generator and battery controlled by a hydraulic system originally designed to operate gun turrets. By March 1941, the Leigh Light was undergoing trials and by August it was in production.

The combination of radar and searchlight enabled a plane to make contact at long range, cut its engines and glide silently toward the target, then suddenly illuminate it just before swooping in to attack. Often the first inkling the night deck watch had that his U-boat was being attacked occurred when he saw the chilling glare of the beam—too late to get away.

As the value of air cover began to be appreciated in terms both of U-boats sunk and of ships saved, the Royal Navy began providing convoys with planes of their own to supplement the protection afforded by shore-based aircraft. In the summer of 1941, 50 merchant ships were fitted out with fighter planes that could be catapulted from their bows. These came to be known as Catapult Aircraft Merchantmen, or CAM-ships.

The planes were most useful in fending off the German bombers that continued to plague British shipping in the Western Approaches and in the Bay of Biscay. In August they scored their first sure kill when a Hurricane launched from the catapult-equipped *Maplin* shot down a Focke-Wulf Kondor 400 miles out in the Atlantic.

But the catapult planes were limited in their usefulness. Once they were launched, they could not return to the ship. When his mission was completed, the pilot had to find an airfield—if he was close enough to land—or bail out or ditch his plane close to a friendly ship with the hope that he would be picked up.

A more potent and less hazardous successor to the CAM-ship was a small escort carrier that could carry several planes to sea and receive them again after their missions were over. The earliest of these were converted freighters or passenger liners on which a flight deck and a hangar had been superimposed. Later, the escort carriers were constructed from scratch and became a permanent and vital part of the Royal Navy.

As the fall of 1941 began, Germany had almost 200 commissioned U-boats, 80 of which were in action at any one time, and the numbers were growing. Admiral Dönitz kept probing for weak spots in the convoy traffic—in the areas

south of Greenland and Iceland and northwest of Ireland. Stragglers that fell behind or ships that chose to go it alone were more vulnerable than ever.

When Dönitz chose to tackle a convoy head on, his torpedoes could still take a heavy toll. But the risk was now greater, for the U-boats had to penetrate rings of escort ships that were faster, better armed and more effectively coordinated than they had been in the Happy Time, not many months earlier.

Although more U-boats were operational than ever before, Dönitz suffered from a shortage of highly trained submariners. Most of the prewar captains were dead or captured, or had been promoted to shore assignments. The new generation manning the U-boats lacked not only the experience, but also the sense of invincibility that had spurred their predecessors. Now it was the Allied seamen and their officers who had experience on their side; many had survived the sinking of one or more ships to return to sea. They were also benefiting from the growing number of escort vessels coming down the ways.

Furthermore, the Royal Navy finally had been able to form escort groups in which six or eight small warships trained together and stayed together through several convoy missions. This was a vast improvement over the days when each escort vessel in a convoy was a complete stranger to her neighbor and the captains could barely communicate with each other.

At about the same time this change in policy occurred, the British received a further assist from an unexpected source—Adolf Hitler. The Führer's campaign in North Africa depended on seaborne supplies from Italy and Sicily. But those supplies were being choked off by the British Mediterranean Fleet and by aircraft from the small but indomitable British base at Malta. Hitler pressed Dönitz to divert his submarines from the Atlantic to the Mediterranean—first six boats, then four more; finally, on November 22, came the order to transfer the entire operational force to the Mediterranean and the area west of Gibraltar.

Dönitz, who was steadfast in his belief that the Atlantic was the decisive theater of operations, resisted Hitler's decision for as long as he could. He viewed the Mediterranean as a trap from which his U-boats would never be able to escape. He was right, for not one of the 62 submarines that were stationed in the Mediterranean ever made it back to the Atlantic—although they did score some successes, including the sinking in November of the carrier *Ark Royal* and the battleship *Barham*.

With the switch of the wolf packs to the Mediterranean, shipping losses suddenly declined in the north, while the waters off the coast of Gibraltar became the most dangerous in the world for Allied shipping. The area was heavily trafficked by convoys, some bringing raw materials from the Far East and others carrying war supplies around Africa to the embattled British Eighth Army in Egypt. For nine days in December, the Gibraltar area became the arena of one of the most significant convoy battles of the War, one in which new and highly effective tactics for dealing with the U-boats were introduced. On Sunday afternoon, December 14, Convoy HG-76 sailed out from Gibraltar, a rectangle of 32 merchantmen guarded by two protective rings of warships under Commander F. J. "Johnnie" Walker, a crusty and able antisubmarine tactician who had acquired a reputation for being an outspoken maverick. Walker had been passed over for promotion to captain and had spent the first two years of the War tied to a desk. But he had his own ideas about combating U-boats, and by now he was eager to put them to the test.

In October 1941, Walker had been appointed commanding officer of the sloop *Stork* and named senior officer of an escort group made up of his ship, another sloop and seven corvettes. For two months he worked his team to exhaustion. He drilled them in a series of coordinated battle tactics to which he gave the unlikely name *Buttercup*—a nickname for his wife.

Commander Walker's tactics were designed to bring a maximum number of escort vessels and a maximum amount of firepower to bear against the U-boats at night, when they were most likely to attack. Walker knew that following a successful attack a submarine would either remain near the wreck of the ship that had been torpedoed or make off on the surface at high speed to escape the attention of slower escorts. "Operation *Buttercup*," he explained, "is designed to force the U-boat to dive by plastering the area around the wreck with depth charges and by illuminating the most likely directions of his surface escape. Once submerged, the

Standing astride a pair of depth charges, granite-faced Admiral Sir Percy Noble, Commander-in-Chief, Western Approaches, praises men of the H.M.S. Stork after the sloop sank the U-574. Behind Noble, double row of brass buttons gleaming, is Captain F. J. "Johnnie" Walker, the Stork's commander and the War's top U-boat killer. The Stork dropped depth charges, forcing the U-574 to surface, then rammed and sank her.

destruction of the submarine is considerably simplified."

In early December, Walker's group had escorted the convoy from Liverpool to Gibraltar without incident. But reports from the Submarine Tracking Room in London left no doubt that the run home again could be made only through a savage gauntlet. Submarines already converging toward Gibraltar were being joined by others coming down from the Baltic on Hitler's instructions. A decisive encounter with Dönitz' U-boats was about to occur.

Walker's escort group of nine vessels was augmented by nine Gibraltar-based vessels: three destroyers, two sloops, three corvettes and the escort carrier *Audacity*. But after the first four days, only the *Audacity* and the destroyer *Stanley,* formerly an American four-stacker, would remain with the convoy; the rest of the escort vessels would have to break off and return to Gibraltar. A converted passenger ship that had been captured from the Germans, the *Audacity* was equipped with six small single-seater Grumman Martlet fighter planes.

On the second day out, the brief appearance of a German Kondor bomber on the northern horizon let the convoy know it had been spotted. By evening of the third day, an upsurge in German radio traffic made it ominously clear that a wolf pack was gathering.

Just after 9 a.m. on December 17, the *Audacity*'s planes reported their first sighting: a surfaced U-boat 22 miles on the convoy's port beam. Walker swung five of his ships away in pursuit. A corvette made contact with the now-submerged boat and dropped her depth charges—in patterns of 10 instead of the old limit of five. The submarine *U-131* was forced back to the surface, her hull damaged by the depth charges, but still full of fight. Walker's ships immediately brought the submarine under a blanket of fire from their 4-inch guns. The U-boat's deck gun shot down one of the Martlets, reducing the *Audacity*'s complement to five. But the submarine was fatally damaged, and the captain had no alternative but to abandon her in order to save his crew.

Fine weather the next morning assisted the escort in making its second kill. This time a lookout on the *Stanley* spotted a submarine as she tracked the convoy from six miles off. Within one hour's time, depth charges brought the *U-434* wallowing to the surface. As the escort ships raced up, the submarine turned over and sank, leaving her crew struggling in the water.

So far, the convoy was unscathed as it zigzagged west and north in a wide circle at a speed of seven and a half knots. But now came the time for the remaining Gibraltar-based escort vessels, except the *Stanley,* to peel off for home. And the battle had only begun. Two more Kondors appeared, to assess the position and course of the convoy before the five Martlets chased them off.

At sunset another submarine was sighted, but she got away and the escorts returned to their screen, anticipating a sleepless night. As they did so, the *U-574* shadowed the ships. At 3:45 a.m. the *Stanley,* which was patrolling the rear of the convoy, reported "Submarine in sight." A second message warned: "Torpedoes passing from astern." Commander Walker in the *Stork* was nearest to the *Stanley* and turned to assist her. The two ships were exchanging signals by flashing lights when, with appalling suddenness, the *Stanley* blew up. The *U-574*'s torpedoes had found their mark, setting off an explosion in the *Stanley*'s magazines and splitting the hull of the old destroyer as a sheet of fire shot hundreds of feet into the air.

No sooner had the flames from the *Stanley* died away than the night was lighted up again. All of the merchant ships in the convoy, following standard instructions when a ship was torpedoed, had fired their snowflake rockets. Now everyone—including the assembled U-boats—was able to see the entire area. Moments later a dull thud from the front of the convoy revealed that a submarine had scored another hit on a merchantman.

Meanwhile, Walker raced to the area where the *Stanley* had been hit and was rewarded with a solid asdic contact at short range. The *Stork* blanketed the area twice with depth charges and was turning for a third run when the *U-574* rose to the surface 200 yards ahead. She tried to escape by turning in a tight circle. Walker gave chase; the *Stork*'s turning circle was slightly larger than the U-boat's but her 19-knot speed was just enough to give Walker the edge. He kept closing in and firing his 4-inch guns until they could not be lowered enough to keep the U-boat in their sights. "After this," Walker later wrote in his report of the battle, "the guns' crews were reduced to shaking fists and roaring curses at an enemy who several times seemed to be a matter of a few feet away instead of yards."

The fight had gone on for 11 dizzying minutes, and the U-boat and her pursuer had turned three complete circles, before the *Stork* caught and rammed her. As they scraped apart, a final pattern of depth charges, set to explode at the shallowest depths, finished off the *U-574*.

The *Stanley* had been avenged. But morning brought a warning from the Admiralty that three more U-boats were on their way to join the fight. One of them was commanded by Lieut. Commander Engelbert Endrass, who had been first watch officer on the *U-47* at Scapa Flow and now was the reigning ace of Dönitz' undersea fleet.

There were no new attacks until December 21, the eighth night of the convoy, when a Norwegian tanker went up in flames. Walker ordered a *Buttercup* search to starboard, illuminating the area with snowflakes as the corvettes raced in to sweep the area.

The carrier *Audacity* was 10 miles out, on the starboard flank of the convoy. Her commanding officer was senior to Walker, and he insisted on keeping his ship outside the convoy perimeter. Usually a corvette was detailed to protect her, but tonight none could be spared. The *Audacity* was alone and silhouetted by the glare of snowflakes when a U-boat cautiously approaching the convoy caught sight of her. A torpedo from the submarine hit the *Audacity's* engine room, flooding it and bringing the carrier to a standstill. The U-boat drew within point-blank range and put two more torpedoes into the carrier. Within 10 minutes the *Audacity* was gone.

For the British the next few hours were a nightmare of submarine sightings, asdic contacts gained and lost and the almost continuous rumble of exploding depth charges. At one point the sloop *Deptford* sighted a submarine inside the perimeter and rushed to the attack. It was Endrass in the *U-567*. The U-boat dived, but the *Deptford* maintained asdic contact and, with assistance from the *Stork,* delivered pattern after pattern of depth charges. The underwater explosions buckled the hull of Endrass' boat and sank her without a trace.

No more ships were torpedoed that night, although the weary British almost managed to sink one of their own vessels. Shortly before dawn the *Deptford* rammed the *Stork* in the darkness. Both ships suffered severe damage.

Meanwhile, the remaining U-boats had drawn off to wait for instructions from headquarters, and in the morning a new element was introduced into the battle. A four-engine Liberator bomber appeared over the convoy. This long-range plane, known in the United States as the B-24, was one of the first of its kind to come into British service and had been assigned to Coastal Command.

The Liberator had flown 800 miles from its base in England to provide air cover for the convoy. In the three hours that it patrolled overhead, it chased off a Kondor and attacked two U-boats that were lying on the surface. One of the submarines had evidently been damaged during the previous night. Her crew scuttled their craft and scrambled to get aboard the other U-boat while the bomber dropped depth charges around them.

The arrival of the Liberator was the last straw for Dönitz, who had been following his commanders' reports on the running battle with increasing dismay. Convoy HG-76 had been under concentrated attack for a week, and had lost only two of its 32 ships. The cost to the Germans had been five U-boats out of the total of nine that Dönitz had committed to the battle, including the submarine that was commanded by Endrass, who was the most experienced of his remaining captains.

Dönitz ordered his U-boats to abandon the attack against the convoy. Given port-to-port air cover and the kind of scrappy escort that Johnnie Walker had thrown up around HG-76, British convoys were proving too much for the U-boat fleet. In a showdown between submarines and a determined, well-escorted convoy, the submarine had been decisively defeated.

The U-boats needed easier hunting than they were encountering in the Gibraltar area and in the North Atlantic, and Dönitz knew just where to look for it. On December 7, Japan had bombed Pearl Harbor and four days later Germany had joined her Axis partner at war with the United States. With America in the scrap at last, the vast flow of unprotected shipping from the Gulf of Mexico up the Eastern Seaboard of North America as far as Nova Scotia was now fair game for the submarines. In 1942 they turned their attention to it with a vengeance.

AMERICA'S ICY CITADEL

British and American warships assemble in Iceland's sprawling Hvalfjordur harbor before starting out with a convoy for the Russian port of Archangel.

THE BATTLE AGAINST BOREDOM

"Whoever possesses Iceland," wrote the German geopolitician Karl Haushofer in the 1930s, "holds a pistol pointed permanently at England, America and Canada." It was a pistol that Great Britain was quick to seize. In May 1940, with the fall of Denmark, the island's former ruler, Britain raced to take control of this subarctic outpost that lay within easy reach of vital shipping routes, putting ashore a force that soon swelled to more than 24,000 men. But a little more than a year later, when the British troops there were needed for duty in Africa, all but a few were gradually pulled out and American Marines took over—a full five months before the United States formally became involved in the War. Eventually as many as 50,000 Americans were stationed there.

The U.S. defenders of Iceland found themselves in a bleak realm. At the height of winter in the far northern latitudes, daylight lasted only four hours. Gale force winds buffeted men and machines. Heavy rains could transform camps into quagmires. With the weather in mind, the Army issued every GI skis and snowshoes—and an unheard-of five pairs of shoes.

Monotony was the No. 1 enemy, more real to most servicemen than the Germans. Some men flew routine air patrols or patched up damaged ships, but the chief excitement available to most of them was training, building roads, erecting huts or hauling supplies. There were few diversions afterhours, except for letters home, card games or reading. The local girls were none too friendly, the beer was weak, and Scotch cost a dollar a shot—a lot of money in the days when a buck private got only $30 a month.

The Americans made the most of their surroundings. They did their laundry in natural hot springs that bubbled up out of Iceland's volcanic terrain, and paved the streets around camp with crushed lava to combat the mud. And as an indication that they had not lost their sense of humor, they fashioned trees out of empty cans and discarded pipes to decorate the barren landscape, built wooden fireplugs and put up street signs bearing familiar hometown names.

Iceland changes command in 1942 as U.S. Major General Charles Bonesteel (second from left) takes over from British Major-General H. O. Curtis.

On lonely, frigid guard duty in March 1943, a U.S. Marine, shouldering a bayonet-tipped Garand rifle, keeps watch at Fleet Air Base in Reykjavik.

strip of neon that silhouetted ships by night, but the Chamber of Commerce refused to douse the lights lest such a move scare the tourists away. The tourists gathered on the beaches to watch torpedoed ships blazing on the horizon.

Naval authorities often were as perverse as the tourists. To the despair of the British, who—after more than two years of painful trial and error in what one American admiral aptly described as the "laboratory of war"—had virtually driven the U-boats from their coasts, the U.S. resisted all manner of British advice. The Americans were even loath to adopt the tried-and-true convoy system along the Eastern Seaboard. The Navy believed that a weakly escorted convoy was worse than a convoy with no protection at all; contending that it lacked enough ships for proper escorts, it provided none. Most American naval vessels capable of coping with U-boats had already gone north to shepherd convoys on the all-important North Atlantic run from Halifax to Iceland—which were now carrying troops as well as cargo. The remainder were on duty in the Pacific, trying to fend off the Japanese, who were advancing through the Philippines and Southeast Asia.

With all these far-flung commitments, there were only about two dozen vessels in the U.S. Navy available to cover the Eastern Sea Frontier—the official designation for the

THE INFAMOUS LACONIA INCIDENT

On the 12th of September, 1942, the British troopship *Laconia,* a 19,965-ton converted ocean liner, was torpedoed in the South Atlantic by the *U-156,* commanded by Werner Hartenstein. The 2,732 passengers on the ship included 1,800 Italians captured in North Africa, and the families of British colonial civil servants. Hearing cries for help in Italian, and fearing a great loss of life in shark-infested waters, Hartenstein sought to rescue the survivors.

The *Laconia* had already broadcast a distress signal, but Hartenstein augmented it with English broadcasts asking all ships in the area for help. He also notified Admiral Dönitz, who radioed the *U-506* and the *U-507* to join in the rescue. Vichy French authorities in Dakar dispatched the cruiser *Gloire* and two smaller ships.

Meanwhile, Hartenstein rescued 260 survivors, later transferring half to the *U-506.* Another 157 were brought on board the *U-507,* and scores more were placed in lifeboats. The decks of the U-boats were full and the crowded lifeboats were in tow when an American Liberator bomber appeared, circled and departed. A half hour later the Liberator returned and dropped five bombs on Hartenstein's U-boat, ignoring flashing signals, radio messages and a Red Cross flag. (The pilot's later explanation for the attack was that two other Allied ships were in the area and were endangered by the U-boats' presence.)

The *U-156* was damaged and Hartenstein was forced to return his survivors to the water. Nevertheless, Dönitz ordered the other two U-boats to continue rescue operations. On September 18, the submarines rendezvoused with the French ships and 1,200 persons were saved.

As a result of the Liberator's attack, Dönitz ordered all U-boats henceforth not to rescue survivors. In the Nuremberg trial after the War, he was charged with murder for giving this order. Although the tribunal convicted Dönitz of other war crimes, he was acquitted on the murder charge, on the ground that the Allies themselves had waged unrestricted submarine warfare and had rarely rescued survivors.

The sleek Cunard White Star liner Laconia was the second ship to bear the name. The first one was torpedoed by the Germans during World War I.

280,000-square-mile ocean area between the Bay of Fundy and Jacksonville. To use those two dozen ships for escort duty, the Navy argued, would leave such vital harbors as New York, Boston, Norfolk and Charleston unprotected. "The plain fact of the matter is that we have not the 'tools' wherewith to meet the enemy at all the points he is threatening," wrote Admiral Ernest J. King, commander in chief of the U.S. Navy, to a colleague. "All in all, we have to do the best we can with what we've got."

Holding fast to that conviction, the Navy attempted to meet the U-boat menace with hunting patrols—a practice long since discarded by the British. "This is one of the hardest of all the lessons of war to swallow," an Admiralty report noted in an attempt to dissuade the U.S. Navy from pursuing this fruitless tactic. "To go to sea to hunt down and destroy the enemy makes a strong appeal to every naval officer," it added. "It gives a sense of the offensive that is lacking in the more humdrum business of convoy protection. But in this U-boat war, the limitations of hunting forces have made themselves very clear."

Like an adolescent bent on showing his independence of the irksome voice of experience, the U.S. Navy refused to listen. And its persistence in sending out hunting patrols was welcomed by the Germans. "It did not take the U-boats long to work out a very effective routine," Dönitz wrote. "By day they lay on the bottom at depths of anything from 150 to 450 feet and a few miles away from the shipping routes. At dusk they approached the coast submerged and when darkness fell surfaced in the middle of a stream of shipping to deliver their attacks by night." The eager U.S. hunting patrols did not manage to sight, much less put out of commission, a single U-boat until April 14—three full months after the submarines' arrival along the coast.

While the hunting patrols were failing, the U.S. was trying a number of other tactics that the British had also tried and discarded. One was the fabrication of five "Mystery Ships," or Q-ships. Armed merchant ships, their weapons concealed by netting, masqueraded as innocent freighters and trawlers. On sighting a U-boat the Q-ship would fling off her disguise and fire away. The first three Q-ships set out from the New England coast in March 1942. Four days later, a U-boat sank one of them—costing the lives of 148 men. After more than a year, the Q-ships' total achievement was three encounters with U-boats—all of which got away.

Another fruitless scheme was to enlist the aid of commercial fishermen. The idea was the brain child of Commander Vincent Astor, a yachting enthusiast and member of the Naval Reserve. With Navy blessing, he outfitted fishermen from Maine to Florida with two-way radios, and bade them report anything suspicious. But fishermen are an independent lot, accustomed to taking their own good time. When they found the presence of unfamiliar craft worthy of comment at all, they frequently waited so long to convey the intelligence that the submarines had vanished.

Meanwhile, the Germans pressed their attack without letup, aided by an innovation they called the "milch cow." This was a lumbering 1,600-ton U-boat, serving as a mobile storehouse that on a single voyage could supply U-boats with food, spare parts and fuel, thereby doubling from two weeks to four the time each U-boat could remain at sea.

By March the Admiralty was on the point of losing patience. Critical supplies destined for Britain via the U.S. coastal route were not getting through. In an effort to convince the Americans of the importance of adopting convoy formations, the British proposed to send 10 corvettes and two dozen antisubmarine trawlers from their own shipyards, together with a pair of experienced officers who would teach the American novices how to use the escorts to best advantage against the U-boats. The U.S. Navy turned down the offer of personnel, preferring to do things its own way.

The Navy did accept the ships, however—putting them to work on April 1, 1942, in a partial convoy system that was soon to be dubbed the "bucket brigade." Under this system, merchant ships received escort protection by day during 120-mile dashes between harbors such as Jacksonville and Charleston; they then laid over in safe anchorages by night. It was a modest beginning, but a step in the right direction. By May that system had evolved into a proper convoy operation between New York and Halifax, and between Key West and Norfolk. By July it had become an interlocking convoy system extending all the way from the oil-rich Dutch island of Aruba, off the northern coast of South America, to Halifax. Like passengers boarding or leaving a train at a local railroad station, merchant ships could join or leave a convoy at any port along the way. They passed by relay from one escort group to another as they left one port and headed for the next.

Together with beefed-up air coverage, the tardily instituted convoy system yielded dramatic results. Sinkings dropped from 23 in April to five in May, and to zero in July. But by then the U-boats had already caused havoc: in six months more than half a million tons of shipping had been sent to the bottom of the ocean off the American coast.

In the spring and summer of 1942, as the number of sinkings on the Eastern Sea Frontier decreased, the U-boats moved to other killing grounds. They found a fruitful one off the Arctic coast of Russia—along the forbidding route taken by the convoys relaying Lend-Lease goods to the Soviet Union. In this new German offensive, American ships—sailing under British command—were to witness the full fury of war at sea, a fury compounded by some maladroit planning by Allied commanders in the face of enemy tactics.

From high quarters to low, everyone viewed the Russian convoy run with suspicion, distaste or dread. Sailors called it "hell below zero"; even in summer there could be temperatures below freezing and rough seas. Admiral Sir Dudley Pound, Britain's First Sea Lord, called it a "millstone round our necks." With the lengthening days in the far north, casualties rose. In one convoy in mid-March, five out of 19 merchant ships were sunk. And among the spring casualties were two cruisers Britain could ill afford to lose.

Meanwhile, the Admiralty had another worry. British intelligence reported that the Germans had removed several of their big warships—of which the most formidable was the brand-new, 42,500-ton battleship *Tirpitz*—from home base in Germany and berthed them on the Norwegian coast, only a few days' sail from the Arctic convoy route. These warships were supplemented by Luftwaffe planes, also now based in Norway, as well as by the ubiquitous U-boats. Because of the danger, the Admiralty began urging the British government to discontinue the Arctic run at least until fall, when the long nights would return.

But the government had other concerns. Germany had by this time committed 80 per cent of its land forces to the Russian invasion, and Russia was fighting for its life. To Churchill and Roosevelt, the need to sustain the Soviet Union was urgent. They could spare no troops to help the country in its ordeal, but they could contribute war goods—and had promised to do so.

And so the convoys continued into June, with their casualties growing increasingly worse. These reached a culmination with PQ-17, the 17th convoy to leave Iceland for Russia. The PQ-17 journey turned into a debacle that Churchill was later to call "one of the most melancholy naval episodes in the whole of the war."

PQ-17 originated in Hvalfjordur, Iceland, on June 27, 1942, bound for Archangel, Russia. It consisted of 35 merchant ships—22 of them American—carrying $700 million worth of planes, tanks, guns and other war matériel; also along were three rescue ships and two tankers. That was an unusually large convoy, and it had an even larger number of ships to protect it—47 in all. There was a close escort of 21 ships, all British, and including two submarines. There was also a supporting force, which was to travel the convoy's route but remain out of sight. This consisted of seven ships: four cruisers—two of them American—and three destroyers. Finally, there was also a distant covering force of 19 warships that included two battleships, one of them American, and one British aircraft carrier, the *Victorious*; these were patrolling the waters between Iceland and Norway, and were expected to be ready to intercept the *Tirpitz* if she left port.

To the men who were charged with carrying out the mission, such an assemblage obviously meant something important was afoot, and although they knew nothing of the arguments over the political and naval strategy taking place in high quarters, they shared a growing apprehension. Remembering the grim-faced skippers of the escort ships as they awaited orders to sail, Commander John E. Broome of the British destroyer *Keppel,* who was in charge of the close escort, wrote: "They were seamen, they knew jolly well that this floating town they were about to form would fill some 25 miles of nonstop visibility. They hadn't got to be told that enemy U-boats, and planes and warships would take advantage of this."

Once the convoy got under way, misgivings eased for a time. The ships were veiled in welcome fog, and the first four days went by with no sign of the enemy. Three ships had to turn back to port, but not because of attack; one ran aground on the rocks off Iceland and two were damaged by heavy ice floes. Then on July 1 a solitary German plane appeared aloft, "its nose tipped slightly to the water, like some ominous nose-to-sea bloodhound," one British officer later recalled. Tension mounted again. Commander Broome wrote that it "brought a chilly feeling knowing that from now on, visibility permitting, PQ-17 would be plotted on German operational wall maps as well as our own."

The next few days brought sporadic raids from the air, but no damage until early on July 4, when a Heinkel-115 torpedo bomber hit one of the ships; a U-boat finished her off. As the day wore on the air raids subsided, and British ships were astonished to find the American ships lowering their tattered ensigns as if in surrender—only to raise spanking clean Stars and Stripes instead; then the U.S. sailors began to celebrate the Fourth of July with singing and dancing on deck. The British ships joined into the spirit of the occasion; the British cruiser *Norfolk* signaled the American cruiser *Wichita:* "Many happy returns of the day. The United States is the only country with a known birthday." And the *Wichita,* enjoying some comic relief of her own, responded, "We think you should celebrate Mother's Day."

In the evening came a new attack by 25 German planes.

Crewmen paint the American merchantman S.S. Troubadour white to camouflage her from German aircraft after convoy PQ-17, to which she belonged, was ordered to scatter on the Arctic run to Russia in July 1942. With three other ships, she hid among the ice floes three days, blending with the background, until she could proceed to Archangel.

Three were shot down, but three merchant ships were hit—two so badly damaged they had to be sunk. But spirits remained high in the knowledge that the halfway point to Archangel had been reached.

Back in London the Admiralty was enjoying no such high spirits. Unknown to all but a few escort officers, British officials had learned that the *Tirpitz* had eluded surveillance; she was known to be somewhere at sea, and was thought to be heading east, in the direction of the convoy, together with several other German warships. Looking back, it would appear that the Admiralty panicked; in any event, it concluded that the *Tirpitz* and the other German warships were closing in on the convoy, and sent out to the startled escort vessels some new and unexpected orders. Three excited messages came over the wireless in the space of 25 minutes. The first ordered the supporting cruiser force to turn back westward. The second ordered the convoy to disperse and proceed individually to Archangel. The last and fatal message was: "Convoy is to scatter." This meant that the merchant ships were to fan out in all directions.

On the escort ships, officers and men alike were stunned. One of the officers aboard the *Wichita,* actor Douglas Fairbanks Jr., recorded the anger of the crew: "What kind of high command have we that with such great force in operation we cannot fight it out? Have the British become gun-shy? How can wars be won this way?"

Commander Broome, as leader of the close escort, then took matters in his own hands. He sent his six destroyers to lend support to the departed cruiser force in the battle he assumed was about to take place with German warships. Broome left the two British submarines in the convoy area, lest the enemy ships show up there. He ordered the other escort ships to proceed independently to Archangel; a few of them, however, chose to accompany whatever merchant ships they could.

But most of the merchant ships were left to their own devices. Beginning early on July 5, the Luftwaffe and the U-boats pressed a relentless attack that lasted a week. On the first day, 12 of the merchant ships, as well as an oiler and a rescue ship, were hit and went down. On the 6th of July two more merchant ships were sunk; on the 7th, two more; on the 8th, one more; and on the 10th, two more.

The men who leaped from sinking vessels plunged into icy waters coated with flaming oil. If they managed to get into lifeboats, they were still 200 miles or more from land. If they reached shore, they might have hundreds of miles to go before finding a settlement.

Of the 35 merchant ships that had set out for Archangel, only 11 reached the Russian port. Of these, one small group of three ships owed its survival to an officer of one of the escort vessels that had chosen to stay the course. It was his bright idea to paint the ships white to blend with the background of ice, and to further camouflage their topsides with sheets. German search planes flew over them—and thanks to the white paint and a fortuitous fog, did not spot them. The last of the ships limped into Archangel—450 miles from the point where the convoy had dispersed—on July 24, three weeks after the crippling order to scatter. If the convoy had kept to its original schedule, it would have made the entire voyage in 12 days.

When all losses had been tallied, the toll was appalling: 153 men had been lost and 22 merchant ships had been sunk—and with them a cargo of 430 tanks, 210 aircraft and 99,316 tons of miscellaneous war goods. Of the 1,300 men who made it to Archangel—some in their original ships, others picked up by British escorts and Soviet rescue vessels—many were maimed by frostbite, incurred in the icy waters. Two dozen unlucky survivors, having rowed for 10 days in a lifeboat in what they thought was the direction of Russia, landed instead in German-occupied Norway, and ended up in a prison camp.

A final ironic twist came to light later on. At the time the Admiralty was sending out its frantic orders to PQ-17 to scatter, the *Tirpitz* was not advancing on the convoy at all, but had simply moved from one Norwegian port to another. German patrol planes had spotted and then lost track of the aircraft carrier *Victorious* of PQ-17's distant covering force, and Hitler had no intention of exposing his battleship to the risk of air attack.

The only thing to be said for the PQ-17 episode was that it taught a bitter and costly lesson, making clear the necessity of keeping a convoy under the constant vigilance of well-coordinated escort vessels. So long as the ships of PQ-17 had stayed together, only three had come to grief; the debacle occurred after the scattering. It was a lesson that was to be driven home again in the critical months ahead.

THE SEA WAR ON CANVAS

German war artist Adolf Boch painted this surfaced U-boat shelling an armed merchant cruiser with her 88mm gun, a quick-firing, general-purpose weapon.

CAPTURING THE ATLANTIC ACTION

Flames shoot up into the sky from the torpedoed U.S. destroyer *Reuben James* in Lieut. Commander Griffith Baily Coale's drawing of the sinking.

Aboard the destroyer *Niblack* in the murky dawn of October 31, 1941, U.S. Navy artist Griffith Baily Coale saw a rising cloud of black smoke a mile ahead. Moments later there was a tremendous roar and a column of orange flame leaped into the night sky. The U.S. destroyer *Reuben James,* escorting a convoy bound for Britain, had just been torpedoed. Coale's ship rushed to the scene. As the *Niblack*'s men pulled oil-soaked survivors from the freezing water, the artist could hear "cursing, praying and hoarse shouts for help." Coale could not forget the horror: his drawing at left of the blazing destroyer—the first American combat ship to be sunk in the Atlantic—has an immediacy and impact only the luckiest of photographers could have captured.

Scores of artists covered the sea war from both sides, and in many ways their art offers the best record of the fighting's most dramatic moments. A photographer was not always able to catch these events, but often a painter could watch the drama unfold and later put down on either a sketch pad or canvas the scenes that had been burned into his consciousness.

If the artist was commissioned in the Navy, he had additional duties afloat, usually serving as an officer of the watch. When fighting erupted, he rarely got much chance to draw; instead he manned a battle station like everyone else aboard. Only afterward did he go on duty as an artist to set down the conflict from his vivid recollection.

The popular American painter Tom Lea, working aboard the U.S. destroyer *Gleaves* in the fall of 1941 on assignment for LIFE, made it a practice to memorize what he saw on deck; then he went below to make sketches and later produced his finished paintings back home in Texas. "With the water slopping in," he recalled, "you couldn't do watercolor. You couldn't even sketch out there; it was like a bucking bronco."

The paintings by Lea and other seafaring artists enabled thousands at home in America and Europe to experience both the peaks of combat and the tense hours between peaks *(right)* in one of the War's most violent arenas.

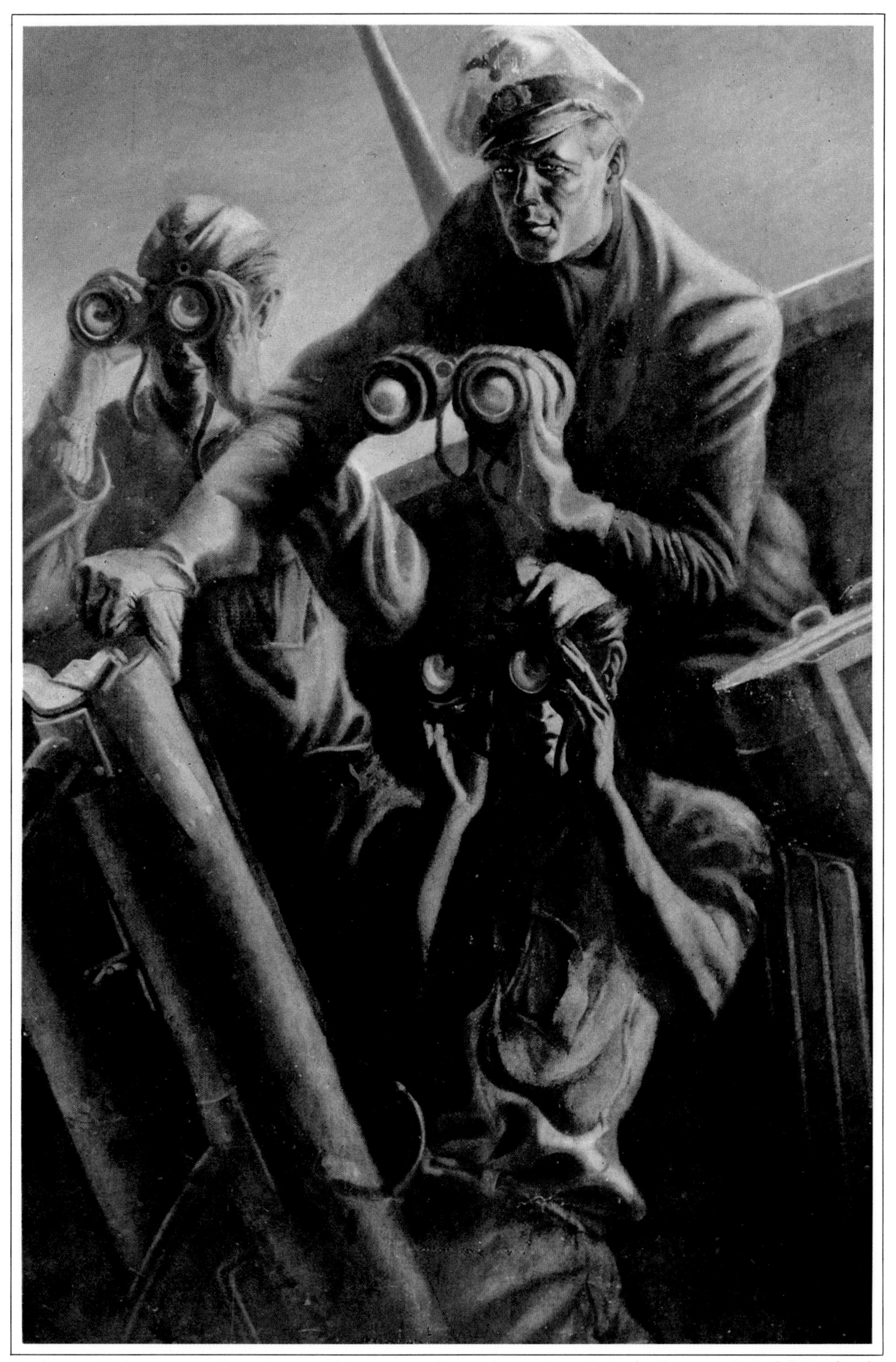

A red-scarved U-boat commander and some of his crew scan the seas for prey in a painting by German artist Rudolf Hausknecht.

"Tossing the Cans" by LIFE artist Tom Lea captures the action aboard the American destroyer Gleaves as members of her crew fire depth charges. The mortar that fired the canisters was known as a Y-gun; it was operated by an explosive charge.

"A Kill in Biscay," painted by U.S. Navy Lieutenant Dwight Shepler, shows a Navy PB4Y depth-bombing a U-boat.

Gunners of the U.S. destroyer Champlin aim at unidentified planes over a convoy in this Dwight Shepler watercolor.

Covered by a comrade with a submachine gun, a rescue party from the U.S. Coast Guard cutter Campbell takes aboard survivors from a sinking U-boat. LIFE artist Lieut. Commander Anton Otto Fischer, who painted the dramatic scene, was on board the Campbell when she attacked the sub at point-blank range in the North Atlantic in 1943.

A sheet of fire runs along the side of the German heavy cruiser Prinz Eugen as she and the battleship Bismarck (left) unleash broadsides against the British

battle cruiser Hood, in a canvas by German artist Claus Bergen. In the May 1941 battle, the Hood was sunk by half a dozen salvos from the two warships.

Rows of Liberty ships, nicknamed "Ugly Ducklings," await final outfitting in California before sailing through the Panama Canal for duty in the Atlantic.

DOWN THE WAYS IN 80 HOURS

Shipbuilding wizard Henry J. Kaiser assembles a prefab model Liberty ship in seven and a half minutes to show how yards could do it in 10 days.

One reason why the Allies were able to win the Battle of the Atlantic was that the United States could build ships faster than Germany could sink them. In 1939-1940 only 102 seagoing ships were constructed in the U.S. But in September 1941, the nation launched a crash program, mustering all of its industrial skills to produce a doughty vessel called the Liberty ship. By the end of 1942, 646 freighters had been completed, 597 of them Liberties, and launchings outnumbered sinkings in the Atlantic for the first time. By 1943, 140 Liberty ships were being launched each month.

At yards all over the country, 1.5 million workers learned to rivet and weld prefabricated components. The 441-foot ship they built—working without letup and at the surprisingly low cost of two million dollars per hull—was a homely adaptation of a British tramp steamer. She could travel 17,000 miles at 11 knots, using old-fashioned steam engines. She was not pretty or fast, but her straight lines and flat planes made her simple and quick to build, and she could carry 10,800 tons of badly needed cargo.

The genius behind this miracle of manufacture was bald and portly Henry J. Kaiser, a 60-year-old California contractor, who had completed the mammoth Boulder, Bonneville and Grand Coulee dams ahead of schedule. The secret to rapid ship construction, Kaiser realized, was to build as much as possible on dry land. Components were assembled all over the country. Freight cars carried them to shipyards, where they were stacked in a "filing system" along the ways where hulls were being built. When a hull was ready, cranes lifted bulkheads, fuel tanks, decks and superstructures into place. Once the hulls were launched, tugs towed them to finishing areas, where engines were installed and all equipment a ship would need at sea was put aboard.

At the peak of the wartime effort, workers constructed one ship in 80 hours and 30 minutes. So fast were the shipbuilders that a joke was told of a woman who stepped up with a champagne bottle, ready to christen a new ship. The keel had not even been laid. "What shall I do now?" she asked Kaiser. "Just start swinging," he said.

Minus its bow, a hull nears completion in a West Coast yard. The largest cranes ever built (background) hoisted the massive prefabricated units into place.

Workers line up to punch out at Kaiser's yard near Portland, Oregon. In shipyards across the United States the day was divided into three eight-hour shifts.

Workers recruited in New York crowd a train station in Hoboken, New Jersey, en route to a Kaiser shipyard in Oregon. Though inexperienced, they were soon welding steel and driving rivets in a race against time.

Ex-waitresses Ina Hickman and May Vincent (left and center) set a shipbuilding record with former seamstress Billie Elliott (right). They welded more plate steel than most of the men who worked at their California yard.

Neatly stacked deck sections and bulkheads for Liberty ships lie ready for hoisting by heavy-duty cranes into hulls taking shape in an Oregon shipyard.

Prefabricated inner floor sections to go into hull bottoms are stacked four deep, ready to be used.

Welders fix ribs of an inner-floor section in place before adding steel sheathing. These 40-ton sections were assembled only a few feet from the ways.

A massive bulkhead is lowered by a crane into the ribbed hull of a new Liberty ship while welders wait in the bilges, ready to secure it in place.

Only two days on the ways, a hull is ready for its first inner-floor section, which will support heavy cargo loaded into the hold for the Atlantic run.

Workers in Los Angeles clear the way for keel number 150, at left, just after launching the Liberty ship in the background. Yards throughout the country competed to find ways to cut corners; awards and bonuses were given to workers for time-saving ideas.

Beach umbrellas shade welders on stove-hot steel decks of a Liberty ship in the summer sun of Southern California. In spite of occasional scorching days, Kaiser located most of his shipyards in California because of the balmy weather through most of the year.

The stern of a Liberty ship is eased into place by cranes, to be welded to the rest of the vessel. The deck of the ship was then fitted into place.

Topping off the hull, the deckhouse superstructure, including the bridge, is added. Skids will now be greased and the ship will slide down the ways.

President Franklin D. Roosevelt (left) and Kaiser, seated in an open car, watch the launching of the Liberty ship Joseph N. Teal, built in only 10 days.

The wives of four wartime businessmen and industrialists smash bottles of foamy champagne on the bows of newly built Liberty ships. Christenings at this yard in Los Angeles were arranged by Terry Lee, who appears in the background of all these pictures. His job was to make sure the bottle broke, even if he had to help swing it. Kaiser's own wife missed once, and the bottle had to be thrown after the hull.

Working around the clock, Kaiser's busy Oregon shipbuilding yard turns out ships under the glare of floodlights. The three Liberty ships in the foregroun

were launched within a single day: one at 12:30 a.m., another at noon, and the third at 4:30 p.m. The midnight christening is shown under way at left.

BIBLIOGRAPHY

Adams, Henry:
1942: The Year That Doomed the Axis. Paperback Library, 1969.
Years of Deadly Peril. David McKay Company, Inc., 1969.
Arnold-Forster, Mark, *The World at War*. Stein and Day, 1973.
Baker, Richard, *The Terror of Tobermory*. W. H. Allen, 1972.
Baxter, James Phinney, *Scientists Against Time*. The M.I.T. Press, 1946.
Bekker, Cajus, *Hitler's Naval War*. Doubleday & Company, Inc., 1974.
Brown, Anthony Cave, *Bodyguard of Lies*. Harper & Row, 1975.
Buchheim, Lothar-Günther, *U-Boot Krieg*. R. Piper & Co., 1976.
Bunker, John Gorley, *Liberty Ships: The Ugly Ducklings of World War II*. Naval Institute Press, 1972.
Cant, Gilbert, *The War at Sea*. The John Day Company, 1942.
Chalmers, W. S., *Max Horton and the Western Approaches*. Hodder and Stoughton, 1954.
Churchill, Winston S.:
The Second World War. Bantam Books.
Volume I, *The Gathering Storm*. 1974.
Volume II, *Their Finest Hour*. 1974.
Volume III, *The Grand Alliance*. 1974.
Volume IV, *The Hinge of Fate*. 1962.
Creswell, John, *Sea Warfare*. Longmans, Green & Co., 1950.
Davidson, Eugene, *The Trial of the Germans*. The Macmillan Company, 1966.
Dönitz, Karl:
"The Conduct of the War at Sea," pamphlet published by the U.S. Division of Naval Intelligence, 15 January 1946.
Memoirs: Ten Years and Twenty Days. The World Publishing Company, 1959.
Eggleston, Wilfrid, *Scientists at War*. Oxford University Press, 1950.
Frank, Wolfgang:
Enemy Submarine. William Kimber, 1954.
The Sea Wolves. Rinehart & Company, Inc., 1955.
Gallery, Daniel V., *Clear the Decks!* William Morrow and Company, 1951.
Hough, Richard, *Death of the Battleship*. The Macmillan Company, 1963.
Hull, Cordell, *The Memoirs of Cordell Hull*. Vols. I and II. The Macmillan Company, 1948.
Irving, David, *The Destruction of Convoy PQ.17*. Simon and Schuster, 1968.
Kemp, Peter K., *Key to Victory*. Little, Brown and Company, 1957.
Kennedy, Ludovic, *Pursuit*. The Viking Press, 1974.
King, Ernest J., and Walter Muir Whitehill, *Fleet Admiral King*. W. W. Norton & Company, Inc., 1952.
Lane, Frederic C., *Ships for Victory*. Johns Hopkins Press, 1951.
Langer, William L., and S. Everett Gleason:
The Challenge to Isolation. Harper & Brothers, 1952.
The Undeclared War. Harper & Brothers, 1953.
Lash, Joseph P., *Roosevelt and Churchill 1939-1941*. W. W. Norton & Company, Inc., 1976.
Lewis, David D., *The Fight for the Sea*. The World Publishing Company, 1961.
Loewenheim, Francis L., Harold D. Langley, and Manfred Jonas, *Roosevelt and Churchill: Their Secret Wartime Correspondence*. Saturday Review Press/ E. P. Dutton & Co., Inc., 1975.
Lund, Paul, and Harry Ludlam:
Night of the U-Boats. W. Foulsham & Co. Ltd., 1973.
PQ 17—Convoy to Hell. W. Foulsham & Co. Ltd., 1968.
Macintyre, Donald:
The Battle of the Atlantic. B. T. Batsford, 1961.
The Thunder of the Guns. W. W. Norton & Company, Inc., 1959.
U-Boat Killer. W. W. Norton & Company, Inc., 1956.
MacNeil, Calum, *San Demetrio*. Angus and Robertson, 1957.
Martienssen, Anthony, *Hitler and His Admirals*. Secker and Warburg (London), 1948.
Mason, David, *U-Boat the Secret Menace*. Ballantine Books, 1968.
Mayer, S. L., ed., *Navies of World War II*. The Hamlyn Publishing Group Limited, 1976.
Mohr, Ulrich, *Ship 16*. The John Day Company, 1956.
Monsarrat, Nicholas:
Breaking In, Breaking Out. William Morrow & Company, Inc., 1971.
Three Corvettes. Ballantine Books, 1962.
Morison, Samuel Eliot:
History of United States Naval Operations in World War II. Little, Brown and Company.
Volume I, *The Battle of the Atlantic*. 1950.
Volume X, *The Atlantic Battle Won*. 1968.
Noli, Jean, *The Admiral's Wolf Pack*. Doubleday & Company, Inc., 1974.
Parsons, Iaian, ed., *The Encyclopedia of Sea Warfare*. Thomas Y. Crowell Company, 1975.
Pope, Dudley, *The Battle of the River Plate*. William Kimber, 1956.
Potter, E. B., and Chester W. Nimitz, eds., *Sea Power: A Naval History*. Prentice-Hall, Inc., 1960.
Preston, Antony, *An Illustrated History of the Navies of World War II*. The Hamlyn Publishing Group Limited, 1976.
Price, Alfred, *Aircraft versus Submarine*. Naval Institute Press, 1973.
Raeder, Erich, *My Life*. United States Naval Institute, 1960.
Rayner, D. A., *Escort*. William Kimber, 1955.
Reisenberg, Felix, Jr., *Sea War*. Rinehart & Company, Inc., 1956.
Reynolds, Clark G., *Command of the Sea*. William Morrow & Company, Inc., 1974.
Richards, Denis, and Hilary St. George Saunders, *Royal Air Force 1939-1945*. Her Majesty's Stationery Office, 1974.
Robertson, Terence:
Night Raider of the Atlantic. E. P. Dutton & Co., Inc., 1956.
Walker, R.N. Evans Brothers, 1956.
Rogers, Stanley, *Enemy in Sight!* Thomas Y. Crowell Company, 1943.
Rohwer, J., and G. Hümmelchen, *Chronology of the War at Sea*. Vol. One: 1939-1942, translated from the German by Derek Masters. Arco Book Publishing Company, Inc., 1972.
Rohwer, Jürgen, *Die U-Boot Erfolge der Achsenmachte 1939-1945*. J. F. Lehmanns, 1968.
Roskill, S. W.:
The War at Sea (3 vols.). Her Majesty's Stationery Office, 1954-1961.
White Ensign. United States Naval Institute, 1960.
Schaeffer, Heinz, *U-Boat 977*. W. W. Norton & Company, Inc., 1952.
Seth, Ronald, *The Fiercest Battle*. Hutchinson & Co., Ltd., 1961.
Sherwood, Robert E., *Roosevelt and Hopkins*. Harper & Brothers, 1948.
Shirer, William L.:
The Rise and Fall of the Third Reich. Simon and Schuster, 1960.
The Sinking of the Bismarck. Random House, 1962.
Showell, J. P. Mallmann, *U-Boats Under the Swastika*. Ian Allan Ltd., 1974.
Taylor, Teltord, *The Breaking Wave*. Simon and Schuster, 1967.
Thursfield, H. G., ed., *Brassey's Naval Annual 1948*. The Macmillan Company, 1948.
Tucker, Gilbert Norman, *The Naval Service of Canada*. King's Printer, 1952.
Von der Porten, Edward P., *The German Navy in World War II*. Thomas Y. Crowell Company, 1969.
Waters, John M., Jr., *Bloody Winter*. D. Van Nostrand Company, 1967.
Watts, Anthony J., *The U-Boat Hunters*. Macdonald and Jane's, 1976.
Williams, E. T., and Helen Palmer, eds., *The Dictionary of National Biography 1951-1960*. Oxford University Press, 1971.
Wilson, Theodore A., *The First Summit*. Houghton Mifflin Company, 1969.
Winn, Godfrey, *P.Q. 17*. Hutchinson & Co., no date.
Winton, John, ed., *The War at Sea 1939-1945*. Hutchinson of London, 1967.
Woodward, David, *The Secret Raiders*. W. W. Norton & Company, Inc., 1955.

ACKNOWLEDGMENTS

The index was prepared by Mel Ingber. The editors also wish to thank William J. Armstrong, Ph.D., History Office, U.S. Naval Air Systems Command, Washington, D.C.; Commander Robert Aubrey, D.S.C., R.N., Ringwood, Hampshire, England; Richard Baker, St. Albans, Hertfordshire, England; Lieselotte Bandelow, Ullstein, Berlin; John D. Barnett, Combat Art Collection, Department of the Navy, Washington, D.C.; Jochen Brennecke, Düsseldorf; Lothar-Günther Buchheim, Feldafing, Germany; R. M. Coppock, Ministry of Defense, Naval Historical Branch, London; Captain Kurt Diggins (Ret.), Director, Deutsches Marine Institut, Bonn-Bad Godesberg, Germany; Grand Admiral Karl Dönitz, Aumühle, Holstein, Germany; Detmar H. Finke, Chief, General Reference Branch, Historical Services Division, Center of Military History, Department of the Army, Washington, D.C.; Ulrich Frodien, Süddeutscher Verlag, Bilderdienst, Munich; Marylou Gjernes, Curator, Center of Military History, Department of the Army, Washington, D.C.; Charles R. Haberlein Jr., Photographic Section, Curator Branch, Naval History Division, Department of the Navy, Washington, D.C.; Commander Stephen Harwood, M.A.R.N., Portsmouth, England; Dr. Matthias Haupt, Bundesarchiv, Koblenz, Germany; Agnes F. Hoover, Photographic Section, Curator Branch, Naval History Division, Department of the Navy, Washington, D.C.; Geraldine Judkins, Operational Archives Branch, Naval History Division, Department of the Navy, Washington, D.C.; Dr. Roland Klemig, Bildarchiv Preussischer Kulturbesitz, Berlin; Judy Koontz, Operational Archives Branch, Naval History Division, Department of the Navy, Washington, D.C.; Charles D. Lawrence, Combat Art Collection, Department of the Navy, Washington, D.C.; William H. Leary, National Archives, Washington, D.C.; Marian McNaughton, Staff Art Curator, Center of Military History, Department of the Army, Washington, D.C.; the staff of the Navy Department Library, Washington, D.C.; Commander the Rt. Hon. Sir Allan Noble, K.C.M.G., D.S.O., D.S.C., Bury St. Edmunds, Suffolk, England; Commodore C. P. C. Noble, C.B.E., D.S.C., V.R.D., R.N.R., London; B. Powell, Ministry of Trade and Industry, London; John C. Reilly, Ships' Histories Branch, Naval History Division, Department of the Navy, Washington, D.C.; Professor Dr. Jürgen Rohwer, Director, Bibliothek für Zeitgeschichte, Stuttgart; Professor Dr. Michael Salewski, Bonn; David E. Scherman, Stony Point, N.Y.; Commander R. E. Sherwood, D.S.O., R.D., R.N.R. (Ret.), Wendover, Buckinghamshire, England; Nancy Stephenson, Saffron Walden, Essex, England; Rear Admiral Erich Topp (Ret.), Bonn; Jim Trimble, National Archives, Washington, D.C.; Frank Vicovari, Brewster, N.Y.; Captain J. E. Wolfenden, D.S.C., R.D., R.N.R. (Ret.), Etchingham, Kent, England.

PICTURE CREDITS

Credits from left to right are separated by semicolons, from top to bottom by dashes.

COVER and page 1—Courtesy Lothar-Günther Buchheim.

THE BATTLE'S FIRST VICTIMS: 6, 7—Popperfoto, London, copied by Henry Groskinsky. 8—Ullstein Bilderdienst, Berlin. 9—Popperfoto, copied by Henry Groskinsky. 10—Wide World—UPI. 11—Wide World (2). 12, 13—Central Press Photo Ltd., London.

UNLEASHING THE SEA WOLVES: 16—Maps by Forte Inc. 17—Bildarchiv Preussischer Kulturbesitz, Berlin. 18—Ullstein Bilderdienst. 19—Courtesy Imperial War Museum, London. 20—Mondadori.

ZANY SAGA OF THE ZAMZAM: 24, 25—David E. Scherman for LIFE. 26—*New York World-Telegram,* courtesy The New York Public Library, Astor, Lenox and Tilden Foundations, and David E. Scherman—map by Forte Inc. 27, 28—David E. Scherman for LIFE. 29—The Reverend V. Eugene Johnson for LIFE (2). 30 through 33—David E. Scherman for LIFE. 34—The Reverend V. Eugene Johnson, courtesy David E. Scherman—David E. Scherman for LIFE. 35, 36, 37—David E. Scherman for LIFE.

RAIDERS ON THE PROWL: 40—With kind permission of Lady Harwood, Goring, Berkshire, copied by Henry Groskinsky. 44—Dever from Black Star for LIFE. 46, 47—Courtesy Imperial War Museum.

SUICIDE OF A MARAUDER: 50, 51—Courtesy Imperial War Museum, copied by Henry Groskinsky. 52—Popperfoto. 53—From Dudley Pope, *The Battle of the River Plate,* William Kimber and Co. Limited, 1956, London. 54, 55—Eugenio Hintz; Camera Press Ltd., London, courtesy Imperial War Museum. 56, 57—No credit (3). 58, 59—Radio Times Hulton Picture Library, London—Popperfoto, copied by Henry Groskinsky.

"HAPPY TIME" FOR U-BOATS: 62—Bildarchiv Preussischer Kulturbesitz. 65—U.S. Navy Department, National Archives. 66—Ullstein Bilderdienst; UPI—Süddeutscher Verlag, Bilderdienst, Munich; Ullstein Bilderdienst. 67—Ullstein Bilderdienst, except bottom left, Süddeutscher Verlag, Bilderdienst.

A SUBMARINER'S EERIE WORLD: 70, 71—Courtesy Kurt Diggins, copied by Henry Groskinsky. 72—Bundesarchiv, Koblenz, Germany. 73—Courtesy Kurt Diggins, copied by Henry Groskinsky. 74—Courtesy Hanns Hubmann. 75—Courtesy Kurt Diggins, copied by Henry Groskinsky—Bundesarchiv. 76, 77—Courtesy Kurt Diggins, copied by Henry Groskinsky; Bildarchiv Preussischer Kulturbesitz. 78—Süddeutscher Verlag, Bilderdienst, copied by Henry Groskinsky—courtesy Kurt Diggins, copied by Henry Groskinsky. 79—From Kurt Zentner, *Illustrierte Geschichte des Dritten Reiches,* copied by Henry Groskinsky. 80, 81—Courtesy Lothar-Günther Buchheim. 82, 83—Courtesy Lothar-Günther Buchheim; courtesy Kurt Diggins, copied by Henry Groskinsky—Bundesarchiv.

THE SINKING OF A U-BOAT: 84, 85—U.S. Coast Guard, National Archives, from UPI. 86 through 93—U.S. Coast Guard, National Archives.

VITAL ARMADAS: 97—Popperfoto. 98—Map by Nicholas Fasciano. 103—Fox Photos Ltd., London. 106—Courtesy National Maritime Museum, Greenwich, England, copied by Derek Bayes.

JOURNEYS INTO DANGER: 108, 109—U.S. Coast Guard, National Archives. 110—Fox Photos Ltd. 111—Radio Times Hulton Picture Library. 112, 113—U.S. Coast Guard, National Archives. 114, 115—Camera Press Ltd., courtesy Imperial War Museum. 116, 117—Süddeutscher Verlag, Bilderdienst, copied by Henry Groskinsky. 118, 119—U.S. Navy Department, National Archives. 120, 121—William Vandivert for LIFE.

THE TRIUMPH OF TECHNOLOGY: 124—Popperfoto. 126, 127—Drawing by Nicholas Fasciano. 128—Courtesy Imperial War Museum; Fox Photos Ltd. 129—Courtesy National Maritime Museum, copied by Derek Bayes. 130—Courtesy Imperial War Museum.

AMERICA'S ICY CITADEL: 134 through 137—U.S. Navy Department, National Archives. 138, 139—Walter B. Lane for LIFE. 140 through 147—U.S. Navy Department, National Archives.

THE UNITED STATES AT SEA: 150—Courtesy U.S. Navy, Naval Historical Center, copied by Charlie Brown. 151—Popperfoto, copied by Henry Groskinsky. 152—U.S. Navy Department, National Archives. 153—Studio Sun. 155—UPI. 158—Courtesy U.S. Navy, Naval Historical Center, copied by Charlie Brown.

THE SEA WAR ON CANVAS: 160, 161—Courtesy U.S. Army Center of Military History. 162—Courtesy U.S. Navy Combat Art Collection, copied by Henry Groskinsky. 163—Courtesy U.S. Army Center of Military History. 164, 165—Courtesy U.S. Army Center of Military History; courtesy U.S. Navy Combat Art Collection, copied by Henry Groskinsky (2). 166, 167—Courtesy U.S. Army Center of Military History. 168, 169—Courtesy U.S. Army Center of Military History, copied by Henry Groskinsky. 170, 171—Courtesy National Maritime Museum. 172, 173—Courtesy National Maritime Museum; courtesy National Maritime Museum, copied by Derek Bayes. 174, 175—Courtesy U.S. Army Center of Military History.

THE FINAL ROUND: 178—Graph by John Drummond, background, William Vandivert for LIFE. 181—Courtesy Imperial War Museum—U.S. Coast Guard, National Archives. 183—U.S. Navy Department, National Archives; courtesy National Maritime Museum, copied by Derek Bayes. 184—U.S. Navy Department, National Archives. 185—U.S. Navy Department, National Archives—Copyright © 1945, 1949 by the Curtis Publishing Company, Copyright © 1951 by Daniel V. Gallery. Reprinted by permission of Harold Matson Company, Inc.; U.S. Navy Department, National Archives. 187—Courtesy Imperial War Museum.

AN OUTPOURING OF SHIPS: 190, 191—UPI. 192—Wide World. 193—John Florea for LIFE. 194—Courtesy The Henry J. Kaiser Historical Library. 195—Wide World (2). 196—John Florea for LIFE. 197—Lawrence Barber, *The Portland Oregonian*—Hansel Mieth for LIFE. 198—UPI—Wide World; John Florea for LIFE. 199—UPI—Wide World (2). 200—U.S. Navy Department, National Archives. 201—California Shipbuilding Corporation (4). 202, 203—Ralph Vincent, *The Portland Journal.*

INDEX

Numerals in italics indicate an illustration of the subject mentioned.

Printed in U.S.A.